Meditations
on the
Rosary

Scripture, Psalms, Illustration, Guided Imagery

SANDRA ENDERS

WESTBOW
PRESS®
A DIVISION OF THOMAS NELSON
& ZONDERVAN

WestBow Press books may be ordered through booksellers or by contacting:

WestBow Press
A Division of Thomas Nelson & Zondervan
1663 Liberty Drive
Bloomington, IN 47403
www.westbowpress.com
1 (866) 928-1240

ISBN: 978-1-9736-0214-9 (sc)
ISBN: 978-1-9736-0215-6 (hc)
ISBN: 978-1-9736-0213-2 (e)

Library of Congress Control Number: 2017913511

Print information available on the last page.

WestBow Press rev. date: 8/24/2017

To Mom, who taught me what it means to be a Christian!

On judgment: No two people ever have the same experiences in life. There is only One who maintains the right to judge another.

On learning: The most profound learning comes from God's revelations within us.

On forgiveness: The ability to forgive yourself, as well as others, is a precious gift to acquire.

On God's grace: The brightest of human intelligences, all the greatest of charisma, and all the money in the world all pale greatly against the smallest piece of His grace.

Contents

Preface

This writing came together after many years of exploring different areas that intersect psychology and spirituality. The practice of self-introspection and the relationship it has with the human belief system is an underlying theme throughout the text. The distinction between belief in an outside divine power and belief in the psychological self can be difficult to understand, but it is a fascinating area of study. Perhaps it is the unique elusiveness of God and His ability to connect to the human mind, both so intangible, mixed with the inability to reveal its workings, that make it so fascinating.

Renee Descartes, in the early seventeenth century, argued that the mind interacts with the body at the pineal gland. He called this area the *seat of the soul* because it appeared to be the only unitary part of the human body. Of course, we have since discovered that the pineal gland does in fact have two hemispheres, and science has yet to identify any particular area of the brain that houses the mind or the soul. But the human mind—and humans are the only animal that is believed to have one—is the essence of what it means to have consciousness of the self. And the spirit, or the soul, is what it means to be human. The concept of belief, and the mysteries of the brain, and even more alluring, consciousness itself, have been a topic of interest for me throughout my life. This book is a result of pondering that relationship for many years.

The book takes the reader through the mysteries of the rosary using over fifty passages of scripture, five psalms, twenty illustrations, and twenty guided imagery scripts. It can be used for individual meditation or prayer practice but is also ideal for Christian group work or one-on-one for pastoral counselors, coaches, or therapists to foster psycho-spiritual growth and development. The guided imagery scripts should be read slowly, using proper tone, inflection, and pace of voice to help create awareness of the surrounding environment, and to encourage interaction with characters in the scene. Comfortably read, scripts run approximately fifteen to twenty minutes long and are designed to be interchangeable, with four basic inductions offered and twenty distinct bodies focused on the mysteries. All twenty scripts have the same closing. By using the senses, the imagery brings the reader or listener into the context of the actual event in Jesus's life and attempts to create direct interaction with the event and/or character. The writings are meant to foster psycho-spiritual growth, initiate personal development, or aid in creating desired positive change in the person.

Chapter 1 looks at defining *meditation* and distinguishing it as a broad generic term. The chapter then discusses distinct differences between meditation, prayer, guided imagery, and hypnosis. These interventions are often used in creating change and healing in both clinical or nonclinical settings. The general differences are important to distinguish because they can be used with both belief in an outside divine source and also with belief in the self. And both beliefs are important to create change.

Chapter 2 rolls out the origins, history, and meaning of the most holy rosary. The rosary is a Christian prayer exercise that surveys the life of Jesus and is most popular in Catholicism. The goal of writing the twenty visual imagery scripts was to combine the four intervention methods with the many Christian virtues (called fruits of the mysteries) found in the traditional rosary prayer routine. It is an attempt to increase insight into the subconscious self and delve into the mind, as well as attract outside energy and divine intervention during the meditations.

Chapter 3 covers the five joyful mysteries. The theme of this section is on angels and gratitude. It offers five guided imagery scripts on the annunciation, the visitation, the nativity, the presentation, and finding Jesus in the temple. Some Christian mysteries (virtues) that arise here are humility, purity, truth, wisdom, and love for others.

Chapters 4 looks at the sorrowful mysteries. The theme here is on redemption and forgiveness. This section offers guided imagery scripts on the agony in the garden, the scourging at the pillar, the crowning of thorns, carrying the cross, and the crucifixion. Some Christian mysteries (virtues) that arise here are mortification, contempt, salvation, patience, and contrition.

Chapter 5 covers the glorious mysteries. Here the theme's focus is on faith and heaven. It offers five guided imagery scripts of the resurrection, the ascension, the Holy Spirit descending, the assumption, and Mary's crowning. Some Christian mysteries (virtues) that arise here are faith, perseverance, heaven, holy wisdom, and devotion to Mary.

The sixth and final chapter investigates the luminous mysteries. The theme in this section is peace and salvation. This section offers five scripts on the baptism of Jesus in the Jordan, the wedding at Cana, Jesus's proclamation of the kingdom of God, the transfiguration, and the institution of the Eucharist. Some Christian mysteries (virtues) that arise here are the Holy Spirit, trust in God, repentance, holiness, adoration, and intervention through Mary.

All scripture verses used in this writing were taken from the New American Bible Revised Edition (NABRE), the only translation currently approved for Mass in the Catholic dioceses of the United States and the Philippines. It was first published in 1970, stemming from the Confraternity of Christian Doctrine (CCD) initiated in response to Pope Pius XII's *Divino afflante Spiritu* encyclical in 1943, which called for new translations of the Bible from the original languages, instead of the Latin. The CCD met from 1941 to 1969, and this resulted in the New American Bible and the move away from the Latin translation. This change coincided with the liturgical principles and reforms of the Second Vatican Council (1962–1965).

The work of the NABRE originated out of the Vulgate, the fourth-century Latin translation that became the Catholic Church's official Latin version of the Bible during the sixteenth century, an outcome from the Council of Trent (1545–1563). Saint Jerome (AD 347–420) is credited with the original translation of the Vulgate. He was commissioned by Pope Damasus to revise the *Vetus Latino*, which was an unorganized collection of biblical texts written in Old Latin. The Vulgate was the first single consistent Latin text translated from the original tongues. By the thirteenth century, it had become the most commonly used version until the move to the New American Bible in the twentieth century, and revised to the NABRE in 2011.

A basic structure of the rosary and the prayers used are included as an appendix. All scriptural passages are included in an appendix. A list of liturgical dates related to the mysteries are also included as an appendix for use in planning for special prayer services and devotions.

The twenty illustrations throughout the book are by Paul Gustave Louis Christophe Doré. Doré was born in Strasbourg, France, in 1832, and died at fifty-one in Paris. Although he was an artist, printmaker, illustrator, and sculptor, he worked primarily with wood engraving. In 1856, he produced illustrations for *The Legend of The Wandering Jew*, which held some anti-Semitic views of the time. He also illustrated an edition of Edgar Allan Poe's *The Raven*. The French government granted him a Chevalier (Knight) de la Legion d'honneur in 1861, from the National Order of the Legion of Honour, the highest French order of merit for military and civil merits, established in 1802 by Napoléon Bonaparte. His illustrations for the Bible that are used in this book were completed in 1866, and Doré had a major exhibit of his work in London soon after, which led to the foundation of the Doré Gallery on Bond Street in the city. He completed a major work in 1872, using 180 engravings, called *London: A Pilgrimage*, illustrating sites throughout the city. But although it received commercial success, the work was not well received by the art critics, who were concerned that Doré seemed to capture too much of the poverty in certain parts of London. The twenty illustrations are listed as an appendix.

1
On Meditative Interventions

The verb *intervene* can be used to describe differing actions, such as intruding, separating, dividing, or interfering, just to name a few. The noun *intervention* can also conjure up various differing visuals, such as mediation, intercession, judgment, or adjustment. Or it can mean an unexpected gathering of family or friends, in an attempt to influence a person to get needed help in a problem area such as an addiction. The concept is often used in health and medicine to describe treatment. In this writing, it refers to a specific practice that can initiate change or healing in a person's life. It can be anything from dealing with a broken marriage, to changing a career in midlife, to getting through grief, to overcoming cancer. The twenty scripts found throughout the book were created to encourage personal insights, change, or healing, and they all mix the following types of interventions. Therefore, the first chapter attempts to define the four as *meditation, prayer, guided imagery,* and *hypnosis.* The scripts are useful in that they use various senses such as auditory and visual as well as body-relaxation methods to encourage contemplation or inner unconscious thoughts to rise to the surface. The strength lies in the fact that that the scripts are placed within the context of the events from the life of Christ taken from the most holy rosary, one of the most powerful spiritual interventions known to humanity and documented throughout history.

Meditation
The English word *meditation* comes from the Latin word *meditārī,* which carries a broad range of meanings including to think, ponder, study,

contemplate, reflect on, or practice. The Hebrew word from the Old Testament was *hāgâ*, which was translated into Greek as *melete*; this Greek word was then translated to Latin as *mediatio/meditari*. The Tibetan word for meditation is *gom*, meaning to become familiar with or to train the mind in states of consciousness, such as compassion, understanding, humility, perseverance, etc. The word used in Buddhism and Hinduism is *dhyāna*, which comes from the Sanskrit root *dhyai*, meaning to contemplate.

Meditation can mean engagement in contemplation or reflection, as in the goal of personal introspection. It can mean clearing the mind completely from thoughts of the past or future with an attempt to stay in the present moment, a goal of mindfulness practice. Or it can be focused on changing something in the future, as with guided imagery or hypnosis. The attempt can be an intercessionary request, as in prayer for another person, or prayer to God through another person, such as through a saint. There are various meanings to the word today. However, in general, all refer to it as *a practice of the individual to train the mind, through mental exercise and detached observation, to reach a heightened state of awareness or a particular mode of consciousness.*

The meaning of meditation is determined by the context it is used in, and it is often attached to the particular religious or spiritual dimension that it was founded in. It is a broad, generic term that encompasses many concepts and practices. It can be a sacred exercise worked in conjunction with an outside higher power, or it can be a completely secular practice focused on the inner cognitive thoughts of the individual. Whether it is used with or without a god, it always involves an internal effort to self-regulate the mind or alter consciousness in some way.

The general concept of meditation in today's world usually conjures up a spiritual aspect to it, whether based on traditional Eastern or Western beliefs, or any of the large array of pop-culture New Age philosophies that are now found. And although it is not necessary to meditate, most of the religious and philosophical origins of the practice usually promote a cleansing of the individual's ethical and moral behaviors, with the goal of clarifying the mind. Most meditation interventions are centered on holistic healing and viewed within the wider context of the person's life. Disordered ethical and moral practices will affect the intended results of the practice, although some modern psychological and medical approaches may downplay the necessity of such. The promotion of virtuous character development has always been at the heart of meditation practices, just as the blending of mind, body, and spirit has been.

One basic distinction should be made between the methods: the difference between striving for an outside divine power to intervene and a self-help approach relying on the individual power alone. Some modalities stress one way or another, and some can rely on both. The four basic categories of meditation practices discussed below arose out of both the Eastern philosophy of Hinduism and Buddhism as well as Western thought based on Abrahamic origins.

Reflective Meditation

Reflective meditation is also known as analytical or discerning meditation. It is a disciplined form of thought that focuses on a specific question, event, or theme. In Eastern tradition (Hinduism, Buddhism, Jainism, Daoism), the goal is for the individual to reach a state of personal enlightenment. This is done by first emptying the mind. In Christianity, reflective meditation is called contemplative prayer; the goal is to understand and know Jesus intimately, and the focus is often on the events of His life. More on reflective forms is discussed under prayer.

Concentration Mantra Meditation

Concentrative forms of meditation focus on a single action, a visual, or most often a sound, which is called a *mantra*. A mantra is a syllable, word, or sound, usually without any particular meaning, which is repeated for the purpose of focusing the mind. In Eastern cultures, mantras have been used in Hinduism, in Buddhism (especially Tibetan), as well as in Jainism, Sikhism, and Daoism (Taoism). It has been debated whether the word or sound itself is important due to the vibration it releases; some argue that the mantra is merely a tool to focus the mind. Transcendental meditation (TM) comes from the ancient Vedic tradition of India, although Maharishi Mahesh Yogi revitalized the practice and brought it to America during the 1960s. The practice involves repeating a specific sound or mantra over and over, which is usually a designated sound of the instructor. During TM, thoughts are said to be transcended and replaced with pure consciousness, considered to be the state of total stability and order.

In Christianity, mantra meditation closely resembles the spiritual exercises of chant and litany. The chant is an unaccompanied melodic line that is sung in sacred ritual. The Gregorian chant is one of the most popular. It arose during the ninth and tenth centuries, although the roots of the practice can date back to early Christianity. This chant eventually became the dominant chant in the Roman Rite and Christian West, and it was the official music of the Christian liturgy. The litany can also be considered a mantra meditation, which consists of a series of invocations followed by a repeated response. The Divine Mercy Litany is a popular Christian litany, which was developed by Saint Maria Faustina in the early twentieth century. Christian contemplative prayer also uses a mantra, usually a designated word, that is used to bring the thoughts back from wandering away from the goal of union with God.

Somatic Practices

Somatic meditation stresses the senses and body energies over the mind and thoughts. Although it is strongly considered a mind-body approach, it often uses practices that stimulate the body more than the mind, in contrast to other forms of meditation. Western practices focus on the embodied self and consciousness that is accessed through emotions, senses, and intuition. Two popular Western somatic forms are yoga and dance. Two others that will be looked at in more depth later are guided imagery and hypnosis.

In Eastern philosophy, somatic forms concentrate more on the body's energy fields, meridian points, and chakra fields, rather than on the senses and feelings. Two popular forms of martial arts that are considered somatic meditation are tai chi and qigong. Both focus on the movement of the body. The goal is to circulate the inner energies, live in harmony with nature, find inner peace, and unify the body and mind as one.

Mindfulness

The word *mindfulness* was initially translated into English from Pali and Sanskrit, two of the Indo-Aryan languages. The concept arose out of the philosophy of Buddha, founder of the Buddhist religion in India, present-day Nepal, during the fifth century BC. *Karma* in Buddhism is the force that drives the cycle of suffering and rebirth for each being. Suffering is caused by craving, and suffering ends when craving ends. A strong guiding principle is the *middle way* or *middle path*—the practice of non-extremism, or the path of moderation away from the extremes of self-indulgence and self-mortification. It is considered necessary on the path to enlightenment, called *nirvana*. The practice strives to maintain attentive awareness of the current moment and being fully present in reality, which completely conflicts with delusion. It maintains calm awareness of one's bodily functions, emotions, and feelings, and one must be similarly aware of any objects of consciousness, such as thoughts and perceptions.

Like the Buddhist (Zen) practice, *mindfulness psychology* is the process of intentionally bringing one's awareness to the internal and external experiences occurring in the present moment; however, it also stresses the need to be accepting and nonjudgmental. It focuses on pondering while observing the ongoing stream of stimuli being experienced at the time, such as thoughts, emotions, sights, sounds, and body sensations. It does not apply critical thought or judgment; one only considers one's simple awareness. Mindfulness is distinctly different than a focus-based approach, such as the mantra concentration in TM, which arose out of Hinduism. TM directs the participant to restrict the focus to one particular stimulus. Mindfulness conflicts with TM because it offers awareness of constantly changing internal and external stimuli as it arises.

Today mindfulness meditation is used in many medical treatment plans, and it is often found in addiction and cancer recovery programs. The well-known mindfulness-based stress reduction (MBSR) training program was first developed by Jon Kabat-Zinn in the late 1970s in the medical school at the University of Massachusetts. The program creates an awareness of the unity between mind and body and the effect that unconscious thoughts, feelings, and behaviors can have on mental, physical, and spiritual health. By easing the stress, it has the potential to increase the immune system's ability to ward off disease. This process increases self-efficacy and enhances one's ability to more easily cope with cues and stimuli interrupting the automatic response cycle, decreasing the need to alleviate emotional discomfort with maladaptive behaviors. The therapeutic goal of mindfulness training is to enhance awareness so one is able to *respond* to situations rather than *react* to them.

Prayer

The word *prayer* comes from the Latin word *precari*, which means to ask earnestly, beg, or petition. It is a request or act that seeks to activate a relationship with a sacred supernatural being of worship through deliberate communication. Prayer is a form of meditation. Three distinctions or stages have been characterized for prayer. The most basic is vocal prayer, such as a group worship recitation of the Lord's Prayer. Reflective meditation is a more structured method and can involve visual and mental focus on a certain aspect, such as reciting the rosary and dwelling on the mysteries. A higher stage of prayer would be contemplative prayer, considered being close to or in union with God. Four common styles of prayer are *worship, guidance, petition,* and *intercession.*

Prayer of Worship

One central theme in the Abrahamic biblical scriptures of the Old Testament was the worship to the one god, Yahweh. This was a new kind of thinking in ancient times, as most cultures practiced polytheistic practices with worship to many gods. Later Jesus told us clearly that praising God with homage and adoration is the most important commandment of all.

> "Teacher which commandment in the law is the greatest?" He said to him, "You shall love the Lord, your God, with all your heart, with all your soul, and with all your mind. This is the greatest and the first commandment." (Matthew 22:36–38)

This form of prayer also includes thanking Him for His mercy and all the gifts and blessings one has received.

> Praise the LORD, for he is good; for his mercy endures forever; Praise the God of gods; for his mercy endures forever; Praise the Lord of lords; for his mercy endures forever. (Psalm 136:1-3)

Prayer of Guidance

In following God's plan, one often asks to be continuously directed in life. Sometimes two roads may lay ahead, both righteous and just, but the road is not clear and it is difficult to decide. Prayer and meditation often move one to decide. Or one may choose to request that He change the direction of an upcoming happening, as Jesus did at the garden of Gethsemane, although it was denied. "After withdrawing about a stone's throw from them and kneeling, he prayed, saying, 'Father, if you are willing, take this cup away from me; still, not my will but yours be done'" (Luke 22:41–42).

Prayer of Petition

Asking for what we want or need is a prayer of faith or petition, with humility and trust that he will do what is best. This includes asking for forgiveness or contrition. It is important that you ask for your request at the time that you are praying, and truly believe you will receive it. Your faith is substantive and tangible; however, it is unseen, although you can still truly believe it is real. But God is eternal, with no past or present or context of time or place. We, however, are mortal temporal beings who live in the context of time and place. When you pray in true faith, God does give you what you prayed for, and if not, something else even better arises. "Faith is the realization of what is hoped for and evidence of things not seen" (Hebrews 11:1).

It is not always revealed when you will get your prayer answered. He will answer it in His own time, but it is your faith that brings it to you. "Therefore I tell you, all that you ask for in prayer, believe that you will receive it and it shall be yours" (Mark 11:24).

Prayer of Intercession

Intercessionary prayer is found in two forms. One is asking God for help for someone else, whatever his or her needs are. It means that you are acting in prayer on behalf of someone else or something else, for instance a church or government. God cannot answer an intercessionary prayer against the person's will. In many of Paul's letters, he is heard saying that he is praying for the people he is writing to. "I give thanks to my God at every remembrance of you, praying always with joy in my every prayer for all of you" (Philippians 1:3–4). It can also be in the form of prayer to an intermediary, such as a saint or the Blessed Mother. The first intercessory request of Mary to her son was for more wine at the wedding in Cana, an event that initiated his public ministry. When the wine ran out, Mary asked Jesus to help the family. "'They have no wine.' [And] Jesus said to her, 'Woman, how does your concern affect me? My hour has not yet come.' His mother said to the servers, 'Do whatever he tells you'" (John 2:3–5).

Contemplative Prayer

Contemplative prayer is sometimes called *reflective* or *centering prayer* and is most often found in the Abrahamic religions. It is sometimes referred to as mysticism, although it is accepted in most areas of Catholicism. It focuses on the personal relationship with God and based on being in God's presence in solitude. It is a much more passive and receptive form of prayer, rather than active and delivery driven. Quiet, peaceful contemplation with God is the goal.

Contemplative prayer differs from Eastern meditations in various ways. The Buddhist and Hindu methods strive to empty the mind through either repeated mantras or clearing the mind of past and future in order to stay aware in the present. The Christian form uses the mantra or reflection to focus on God. Centering prayer is not meant to replace but to supplement the more verbal, imaginative, and active forms of scriptural prayer.

Three Stages of Prayer
1. Vocal is repetitive and often used in groups.
2. Reflective uses a visual and mental focus.
3. Contemplative is closest to union with God.

Four Styles of Prayer
1. Worship pays homage to the divine.
2. Guidance asks the divine for direction.
3. Petition asks for help with something specific.
4. Intercession prays for someone else or to an intermediary to take the request higher.

Guided Imagery

Guided imagery, also called creative visualization, is a technique of using the mind to create changes, healing, and the life you desire. Through your own imagination and thoughts, you can make the changes needed and achieve what you want to. This concept is based on the belief that the universe, and all matter in it, is a form of energy. Each piece of matter vibrates at different rates of speed, and the vibration determines the denseness of the matter. For instance, a piece of granite is much denser than an animal or a person. Thoughts are extremely light and mobile for transport or changing.

A thought can arise and change in an instant. All change begins with an idea, and forms follow ideas. Nothing can change unless the idea is set in motion to first initiate the change. All energy is magnetic, and so the energy that radiates from a person will be reflected back. This theory is sometimes referred to as the law of attraction. It is similar to positive thinking, but not exactly. Positive thinking is more of a psychological construct based on strictly cognitive thoughts of an individual and a bit slight in comparison. The law of attraction, which much guided imagery is based on, is more concerned with the energy and magnetism of the person within the universe, rather than the psych or thoughts of one individual.

Guided imagery is also similar to the practice of hypnosis where a trained practitioner aids the participant to evoke stimulation of the senses through mental images, which can sometimes be emotionally charged. This process attempts to reenact sensory perception in various categories, such as scents, tastes, sounds, and sights, even reactions to touch, can be accomplished without any stimuli being actually present. If wording is chosen properly, and attention given to the imagined situation, along with increased relaxation of the body, the negative thoughts surrounding the stimuli can be separated from the conditioned response and get severed from the previously attached emotion, and then attached to more positive thoughts.

Guided visualization practice is fairly passive, in comparison to hypnosis. Both methods begin with relaxation exercises, but hypnosis moves on to a more interactive mode, with the practitioner being involved in reprograming the unconscious using strong suggestions or even demands. Guided imagery is more about freeing the mind so it will be open to self-introspection. Both practices can directly influence the autonomic nervous system and create physiological changes. In response, more positive emotions, such as the feeling of relaxation, will then become attached to the stimuli and memories that cause the problem. This means targeting the visual, auditory, tactile, gustatory, or olfactory receptors to provoke the desired emotional response. This technique can be as simple as a teenage boy visualizing a home run at his next high school game or as complex as imagining millions of immune cells on a mission to annihilate cancer cells.

Two forms of guided imagery are active and receptive. The active form is sometimes called voluntary, and the receptive form is sometimes referred to as involuntary. The use of visualization techniques assumes that participation in both voluntary and involuntary ways is necessary for a person to be able to perceive and view him or herself. Active voluntary uses reasoning and problem solving to deliberately generate images. Receptive involuntary creates spontaneous images using sensory perception and is without intent.

The use of guided imagery is generally safe. However, certain conditions may warrant caution to use on your own without a behavioral specialist present. For instance, posttraumatic stress disorder is caused by experiencing a traumatic event, defined as being life threatening. The use of guided imagery for therapeutic purposes may trigger very vivid and emotionally charged images that can be heightened by certain scripts, rather than soothed. Similarly, social anxiety, depression, and other mood disorders can also have a negative effect if not used properly.

Hypnosis

There are various styles and methods that fall under the guise of hypnosis. Division 30 (Society of Psychological Hypnosis) of the American Psychological Association defines clinical hypnosis as:

> a procedure during which a health professional or researcher suggests while treating someone, that he or she experience changes in sensations, perceptions, thoughts or behavior. Although some hypnosis is used to make people more alert, most hypnosis includes suggestions for relaxation, calmness and well-being. Instructions to imagine or think about pleasant experiences are also commonly included during hypnosis. People respond to hypnosis in different ways. Some describe hypnosis as a state of focused attention, in which they feel very calm and relaxed. Most people describe the experience as pleasant.[1]

There are various modalities that can be implemented to delve into the

---

[1] VandenBos, Gary R. (editor), APA Dictionary of Psychology (Washington, DC, American Psychological Association, 2007)

unconscious mind. Each one has strengths and weaknesses, and much of the success is determined on finding the correct fit between the person, the process, and the problem that is being targeted. *Traditional hypnosis* uses simple, direct suggestions to the unconscious mind while the person is in the state of deep relaxation. However, this style is not very effective for people who are critical or analytical thinkers.

Ericksonian hypnosis use short stories or metaphors to make suggestions and bring ideas to the unconscious mind. This is a more powerful and effective method than traditional hypnosis, because it can cut through blockages and resistance to change past suggestions that have been deeply embedded. There are two types of metaphors, *isomorphic*, and *interspersal*. Isomorphic metaphors give direction to the unconscious through storytelling that offers a moral. It draws on a one-to-one relationship between elements of the story and elements of a problem situation or behavior. The interspersal-style metaphor uses an embedded command technique. The hypnotist tells a story that engages and distracts the conscious mind that contains hidden indirect suggestions that are more easily accepted by the unconscious.

Neuro-linguistic programming (NLP) uses suggestions to change the cognitive thought patterns that are creating a problem. NLP is as effective as the experience of the practitioner. *Reframing* is similar to NLP and can be considered a subtype of it. The process is an effective technique for promoting a change in behavior. This process acknowledges that all behavior offers a positive outcome (secondary gain) of some kind even if the method of getting to that outcome is destructive. The outcome is important. However, the behavior that is used to accomplish that outcome can be substituted with another, more productive method.

Subliminal programs use two recording tracks. One track is a cover sound that is heard by the conscious mind, and the second track includes direct suggestion that are heard by the unconscious mind. This method offers varied results depending on the audio level of the suggestions.

2
On the Most Holy Rosary

The term *rosary* originated from the Latin word *rosarium*, meaning crown or garland of roses. Catholic tradition maintains that the rosary was given to Saint Dominic de Guzman (1170–1221) during an apparition of the Blessed Virgin Mary at the Church of Prouille in 1214. This event supposedly transpired on the eve of a major Crusade battle against the Cathar heresy, which at that time was running rampant throughout France. This apparition of the Blessed Mother by Saint Dominic was said to give favor to him with the battle. It eventually developed into one of the largest Marian devotions in the Catholic Church, known as Our Lady of the Rosary. An English nobleman, Simon IV de Montford (1175–1218), funded much of the early Dominican Order, and this site in Prouille became known as the cradle of the Dominicans.

De Montford also led the battle of about forty thousand against the Albigensians at Muret.in Toulouse in the southwestern corner of what is today France. Initiated by Pope Innocent III during the second crusade period, the battle continued for two decades. The goal of the campaign was to eliminate Catharism in France. The medieval Christian Cathars sect originated from a reform movement within the churches of southern France. Although it was a return to the Christian message of perfection, poverty, and preaching, it also held a very dualistic system of worship, rather than the monotheistic Judeo-Christian system. It was deemed heretical by the Catholic Church, and between 1022 and 1163, the sect was condemned by eight local church councils and by the Third Council of the Lateran of 1179. Pope Innocent III offered the lands of the Cathar heretics to any French nobleman willing to take up arms. This Cathar Crusade, sometimes called the Albigensian Crusade, greatly influenced the creation and institutionalization of both the Dominican Order and the later Medieval Inquisition.

Catholic tradition concerning Saint Dominic and the origins of the rosary may be an interesting story. However, a more scholarly explanation might argue that the devotion was more likely a gradual development. There is strong speculation that prayer beads may have been used by the laity to imitate the Liturgy of the Hours recited by the monks who prayed the 150 Psalms daily. Since most of the laity followers of Christ at that time were illiterate, 150 knots on a cord could easily have been used as an early system for reciting the rosary. There has been much evidence suggesting that by the Medieval period, both the Our Father and the Hail Mary were recited using prayer beads. By the thirteenth century, trade guilds of Paris reported having prayer bead makers as members. They were called *paternosterers*, and the beads were referred to as *paternosters*. In time the Hail Mary came to replace the Our Father as the favored prayer. Eventually, each decade was preceded by an Our Father, which resembled the structure of the monastic Liturgy of the Hours.

During the Middle Ages, the book of Psalms, which often included other devotional writings, became popular. These were called *psalters*. These books were used by laypeople and were commonly used for learning to read. This later developed into the *Book of Hours*, which monks and nuns were required to recite. By the twelfth century, this had developed into the *Breviary*, which contained the liturgical texts. These used weekly cycles of psalms, prayers, hymns, antiphons, and readings that changed with the liturgical season. Because the psalters were used by laypeople, although similar using 150 psalms, developed independently in areas. In Ireland, the psalter was highly regarded and was called *Na tri coicat*, meaning three fifties. This three-way division was brought to the European mainland and later developed into the original three divisions, joyful, sorrowful, and glorious.

Art depiction and texts reveal that prayer-counting beads existed long before Saint Dominic and date back to the antiquities era in many parts of the world. It is the mix of meditation with the repetitive prayers that makes the practice so fulfilling to the person praying and to God. This advancement of the rosary devotion, mixing prayer with meditation, began to develop during the fourteenth century. The development of the practice is often attributed to Dominic of Prussia (1382–1460), a Carthusian monk. He named the devotional prayer, the "Life of Jesus Rosary." It was very similar to the method used today, a combination of repetitive prayers along with a background of meditation on the mysteries. Often paintings or drawings of the mystery were included in the practice, just as they often are today. This practice of mixing the three—visual, auditory, and mental focus—has made the rosary one of the most powerful prayer interventions documented through history.

The Blessed Alanus de Rupe (Saint Alan of the Rock), a Dominican priest and theologian (1428–1475), promoted the devotion throughout the fifteenth century. He increased interest by developing the fifteen promises of the most holy rosary of the Blessed Mother. It was said that he had a vision of Jesus urging him to advocate for the rosary. Saint Alan is also attributed with establishing the first rosary confraternities. In 1470, he founded the Confraternity of the Psalter of Jesus and Mary, which contributed greatly to the rosary's popularity.

The Fifteen Promises of the Most Holy Rosary by Saint Alan

1. Whoever shall faithfully serve me by the recitation of the rosary, shall receive signal graces.
2. I promise my special protection and the greatest graces to all those who shall recite the rosary.
3. The rosary shall be a powerful armor against hell. It will destroy vice, decrease sin, and defeat heresies.
4. It will cause virtue and good works to flourish; it will obtain for souls the abundant mercy of God; it will withdraw the heart of men from the love of the world and its vanities and will lift them to the desire of eternal things. Oh, that souls would sanctify themselves by this means.
5. The soul that recommends itself to me by the recitation of the rosary shall not perish.
6. Whoever shall recite the rosary devoutly, applying himself to the consideration of its sacred mysteries, shall never be conquered by

misfortune. God will not chastise him in his justice, and he shall not perish by an unprovided death; if he be just, he shall remain in the grace of God and become worthy of eternal life.

7. Whoever shall have a true devotion for the rosary shall not die without the sacraments of the church.

8. Those who are faithful to recite the rosary shall have, during their life and at their death, the light of God and the plenitude of His graces; at the moment of death, they shall participate in the merits of the saints in paradise.

9. I shall deliver from purgatory those who have been devoted to the rosary.

10. The faithful children of the rosary shall merit a high degree of glory in heaven.

11. You shall obtain all you ask of me by the recitation of the rosary.

12. All those who propagate the holy rosary shall be aided by me in their necessities.

13. I have obtained from my Divine Son that all the advocates of the rosary shall have for intercessors the entire celestial court during their life and at the hour of death.

14. All who recite the rosary are my sons and brothers of my only son, Jesus Christ.

15. Devotion of my rosary is a great sign of predestination.

Confraternities were formal religious organizations dedicated to the rosary, which often attracted women, who, at that time, had few social outlets. The women would gather regularly to recite the prayers of the rosary together, often scheduling the members to take turns, making it a point to have continuous recitation run with no interruptions. Arch-confraternities also began to blossom within the dioceses. An archconfraternity is a confraternity that has expanded to the point that other confraternities adopt its structure and rules.

Canonical erection is the approval of the proper ecclesiastical authority, which gives legal existence to a religious order or confraternity. Administrative requirements for this procedure are indicated in canons 608–611 of the Catholic Church Code of Canon Law. Aggregation, or affiliation, as it is sometimes called, is allowed only by those who have received expressed powers directly from the Holy See. Ordinarily, the bishop of the diocese approves and erects confraternities. A pastor of a diocese church or a superior of a religious house can petition for a confraternity. However, both require the consent of the bishop. A confraternity can be petitioned for a religious order or for a parish. The church pastor usually petitions. However, the bishop can, under certain conditions, delegate a religious order to do so. The Dominican Order has been historically entrusted by the Holy See to erect and oversee many of the Catholic confraternities.

The Hail Mary prayer, or as it is sometimes called, the Ave Maria; is one of the most familiar prayers recited in Christian religions in honor of the Blessed Mother. It includes three unique parts. The first, "Hail (Mary) full of grace, the Lord is with thee, blessed art thou amongst women," embodies the words used by the angel Gabriel in saluting the Blessed Virgin (Luke 1:28). The second, "and blessed is the fruit of thy womb (Jesus)," is inspired by the greeting of her cousin Elizabeth (Luke 1:42), which lends itself the more to the first passage, as the words in Latin (*benedicta tu in mulieribus*) from both passages translate into "blessed are you among women." The petition "Holy Mary, Mother of God, pray for us sinners now and at the hour of our death. Amen" is stated by the official Catechism of the Council of Trent to have been worded by the Catholic Church. Today's Ave Maria, as we now recite it, was written by the Camaldolese monks in the Order de Mercede in 1514. The official recognition of the prayer was acknowledged in the writings of the Catechism of the Council of Trent and finally included in the Roman Breviary of 1568.

In 1474, a German Dominican, Jacques Sprenger (1436–1495), founded the Confraternity of the Holy Rosary. He is credited for originally dividing the mysteries into the three sections, the joyful, sorrowful, and glorious. Pope Pius V (1504–1572) later adopted Jacques Sprenger's version for the official practice in the Catholic Church, which was used until 2002 when Pope John Paul added the luminous mysteries. His papal bull, *Consueverunt Romani Pontifices*, in 1569, created uniformity of the Holy Rosary, endorsing the Dominican Rosary as the standard (15 decades /150 Hail Marys). This document also urged the practice of meditation on the mysteries during prayer. A papal bull today is an official document issued by the pope, although early in the church, it was used for unofficial administration purposes. Its distinction is due to its seal of metal, which is usually lead, and differs from an encyclical that is written to develop the church's teachings, rather than for administration purposes.

Soon after, another book on the rosary entitled *Rosario della Sacratissima Vergine Maria* (1587) by Ven. Luis de Granada, a Dominican friar (1505–1588), was published in Italian. A decade later in 1597 the first recorded use of the word *rosary* appeared in reference to prayer beads. It is said that Alberto de Costello, a Dominican, was the first to use the term *mystery* to refer to the meditations. Alberto attached a mystery to each of the 15 Our Fathers, and maintained 150 sub-mysteries for each Hail Mary. His *Rosario della gloriosa Vergine Maria* was published in 1524 and *Meditationi dei Rosario della Gloriosa Maria Vergine* in 1583.

Saint Louis de Montfort (1673–1716) was a French Roman Catholic priest and third-order Dominican. Montfort is known for his particular devotion to the Blessed Virgin Mary and the practice of praying the Rosary. He wrote *The Secret of the Rosary* and *The Secret of Mary* and was an early writer in the field of Mariology. He also had a special devotion to the angels and began the Daughters of Wisdom Catholic community for women.

Since the sixteenth century, many popes have devoted attention to the rosary, most notably Pope Leo XIII. During his years as pope (1878–1903), Leo XIII wrote twelve encyclicals and five apostolic letters on the rosary, beginning in 1883 and concluding in 1898. His first, the encyclical *Supremi Apostolatus Officio* in 1883, is also known as "On Devotion of the Rosary."

After the Second Vatican Council, Pope Paul VI write two encyclicals devoted to the rosary. His first in 1966, *Christi Matri*, was on praying the Rosary during the month of October. In 1974, he wrote the Mariological Apostolic Exhortation *Marialis Cultus*, also known as "For the Right Ordering and Development of Devotion to the Blessed Virgin Mary."

In 1987 Pope John Paul II wrote the encyclical *Redemptoris Mater*, dedicated to the Blessed Virgin Mary within the life of the church. In 2002, John Paul II, in the twenty-fifth year of his papacy, announced that October 2002 to October 2003 would be dedicated to the rosary. The dedication would be referred to as the Year of the Rosary. That year his apostolic letter on the rosary, the *Rosarium Virginis Mariae*, was published. This document introduced the five luminous mysteries to the rosary, which previously maintained the five joyful mysteries, the five sorrowful mysteries, and the five glorious mysteries. The new *mysteries of light* focused on Jesus's public ministry. This was the first major change to the devotion since the sixteenth century. Pope Jon Paul II called for the changes, or addition, to the rosary, in response to the socio-political climate unfolding around the world. He reasoned that it was in response to three crises in the world. The most basic social institution was under attack, namely the family. The jilt to world peace on September 11, 2001, set off fear throughout America, and for many around the world. And last, the rosary itself was at jeopardy of being forgotten within the Catholic Church. It was John Paul's plea for Catholics to rediscover the rosary.

3

The Joyful Mysteries

Body/Somatic Induction Scripts
Theme: Angels and Gratitude

The Annunciation of the Lord to Mary
The Visitation of Mary to Elizabeth
The Nativity of our Lord Jesus Christ
The Presentation of Our Lord
Finding Jesus in the Temple

The Joyful Mysteries, rightly named, reflect on fruits such as humility, gratitude, poverty, and the joy of finding Jesus. The importance of the angels, celestial beings, on the hierarchy and continuum between God and humanity are also present here. But it is most joyous because it includes the incarnation, God in the materiel world, sent to earth in human form with the birth of Jesus Christ. The focus in these events is on both Mary and her Son, Jesus.

> Who would believe what we have heard?
> To whom has the arm of the LORD been revealed?
> He grew up like a sapling before him,
> like a shoot from the parched earth;
> He had no majestic bearing to catch our eye,

no beauty to draw us to him.
He was spurned and avoided by men,
a man of suffering, knowing pain,
Like one from whom you turn your face,
spurned, and we held him in no esteem.
Yet it was our pain that he bore,
our sufferings he endured.
We thought of him as stricken,
struck down by God and afflicted,
But he was pierced for our sins,
crushed for our iniquity.
He bore the punishment that makes us whole,
by his wounds we were healed.
We had all gone astray like sheep,
all following our own way;
But the LORD laid upon him
the guilt of us all.
Though harshly treated, he submitted
and did not open his mouth;
Like a lamb led to slaughter
or a sheep silent before shearers,
he did not open his mouth.
Seized and condemned, he was taken away.
Who would have thought any more of his destiny?
For he was cut off from the land of the living,
struck for the sins of his people.
He was given a grave among the wicked,
a burial place with evildoers,
Though he had done no wrong,
nor was deceit found in his mouth.
But it was the LORD's will to crush him with pain.
By making his life as a reparation offering,
he shall see his offspring, shall lengthen his days,
and the LORD's will shall be accomplished through him.
Because of his anguish, he shall see the light;
because of his knowledge, he shall be content;

My servant, the just one, shall justify the many,
their iniquity he shall bear.
Therefore, I will give him his portion among the many,
and he shall divide the spoils with the mighty,
Because he surrendered himself to death,
was counted among the transgressors,
Bore the sins of many,
and interceded for the transgressors.
(Isaiah 53:1–12)

The Annunciation of the Lord to Mary
First Joyful Mystery
Fruit of the Mystery: Humility

The annunciation celebrates the announcement by the angel Gabriel to the young virgin that she would become impregnated by God, conceive a male child, and become the mother of the Son of God, marking His incarnation. Incarnation refers to the conception and birth of a sentient being who is the material manifestation of a spiritual entity, or god, whose original nature is immaterial. Gabriel also informed Mary at that visit that her cousin Elizabeth was in her sixth month of pregnancy (Luke 1:26) and that she should visit her. Elizabeth was past her child-bearing years, but her husband, Zechariah, had also been visited by an angel to inform him of Elizabeth's conception of a son.

> In the sixth month, the angel Gabriel was sent from God to a town of Galilee called Nazareth, to a virgin betrothed to a man named Joseph, of the house of David, and the virgin's name was Mary. And coming to her, he said, "Hail, favored one! The Lord is with you." But she was greatly troubled at what was said and pondered what sort of greeting this might be. Then the angel said to her, "Do not be afraid, Mary, for you have found favor with God. Behold, you will conceive in your womb and bear a son, and you shall name him Jesus. He will be great and will be called Son of the Most High and the Lord God will give him the throne of David his father, and he will rule over the house of Jacob forever, and of his kingdom there will be no end." (Luke 1:26–33)

The Annunciation
By Paul Gustave Doré (1866)

The Lord himself will give you a sign; the young woman, pregnant and about to bear a son, shall name him Emmanuel. (Isaiah 7:14)

Induction: Body Scan

Start by finding a comfortable position. If you are sitting, have your feet grounded to the floor. If you are lying down, wriggle your feet and toes for comfort. Rest your arms and hands in a comfortable position, either on your lap or by your side, with hands open, closed, in prayer position, or whatever feels easiest for you. Now take three long, deep breaths, slowly breathing in and out from your lower belly area, in through your nose and out through your mouth. Gently close your eyes and begin to direct your attention to your body. Notice how it feels in this moment. Let yourself relax completely by releasing any areas of tension that you may sense, and feel the weight of your body simply loosening into total surrender. Begin to scan your body, starting from the top of your head and working your way slowly downward, moving throughout your head and into your neck and now releasing tension throughout your shoulders and down into your arms and fingers. Feel the stress and tension floating right out of your body as you scan your entire frame. Imagine the anxiety and all negative energies exiting your body. Now move your attention down your diaphragm and into your stomach. Then move your attention throughout your back area and down to your hips and thigh area, letting all your muscles give up their hold. Now throughout your legs, right down into your toes.

Keep breathing, and as you exhale, let your body relax even more. Continue to take long, slow, deep breaths in and out. Notice the areas of your body that feel the most relaxed, and let this calm and relaxed feeling spread to any areas that may still feel some tension. Imagine your muscles melting into total relaxation, and now clear your mind, free your thoughts, and focus on my voice. You are going to be meeting with Mary and the Angel Gabriel at the annunciation of our Lord.

Context

Envision that you are traveling back in time two thousand years ago to Israel in the Middle East. The Roman Empire has held control for sixty years, and King Herod the Great is tetrarch of Galilee in the province of Judea, and although he is Jewish, he is appointed by Rome to keep the Israelites in place. Times are tense, with the Jewish people being persecuted as they continue to pray for the coming of their long-prophesied messiah.

You are in the small village of Nazareth in northern Israel on the west bank of the Jordan River. It is the home of Joachim and Anna, both from the house of David. Their daughter Mary is there, now in her early teen years. Consider what it may have been like for Mary, so young and unknowing, when God's messenger, the angel Gabriel, appeared to her—the fear and bewilderment she would have experienced.

> And the angel said to her in reply, "The holy Spirit will come upon you, and the power of the Most High will overshadow you. Therefore, the child to be born will be called holy, the Son of God. And behold, Elizabeth, your relative, has also conceived a son in her old age, and this is the sixth month for her who was called barren; for nothing will be impossible for God." Mary said, "Behold, I am the handmaid of the Lord. May it be done to me according to your word." Then the angel departed from her. (Luke 1:35–38)

Now ponder the virtue of humility, the fruit of the annunciation, so unpretentious, yet miraculous event that would eventually change the world. Consider the good news that this unborn child eventually leaves behind for all the world to live by—forgiveness and redemption, goodwill toward others, and no more sacrificial offerings, as this child will be the last sacrificial lamb of God, crucified for our salvation.

Today you are there with Mary when the Angel Gabriel visits her. You are a witness to this miracle. Now ponder for a few moments on what this scene could bring to you today in your life!

(Take a long pause of three to five minutes.)

Reorientation

Now the scene begins to fade away, but his message lingers on in your heart and with all who honor him. Give thanks to God and show gratitude for all that you are, the wondrous life and love that you have around you. When you are ready to leave your peaceful place, you can begin to reawaken your body and mind. Feel your muscles reawakening as you take note of your surroundings and slowly return to the present. Wiggle your fingers and open and close your hands a few times. Wiggle your toes and flex your ankles. Begin to move your arms and legs, and when you are ready, slowly reopen your eyes. Stretch if you desire to, feeling your body becoming fully awake. Now take a moment to sit quietly as you reawaken completely and further ponder the experience.

The Visitation of Mary to Elizabeth
Second Joyful Mystery
Fruit of the Mystery: Love of Neighbor

Mary visited her cousin Elizabeth in Ein Karem after the angel Gabriel informed her of Elizabeth's pregnancy. Most likely Mary stayed for the birth of John. Catholicism holds that the purpose of the visit was to bring divine grace to both Elizabeth and her unborn child, as "he leapt for joy in his mother's womb and was filled with the Holy Spirit" (Luke 1:41) as Mary approached mother and child, and at that moment was cleansed from original sin and filled with divine grace.

> In the days of Herod, King of Judea, there was a priest named Zechariah of the priestly division of Abijah; his wife was from the daughters of Aaron, and her name was Elizabeth. Both were righteous in the eyes of God, observing all the commandments and ordinances of the Lord blamelessly. But they had no child, because Elizabeth was barren and both were advanced in years. Once when he was serving as priest in his division's turn before God, according to the practice of the priestly service, he was chosen by lot to enter the sanctuary of the Lord to burn incense. Then, when the whole assembly of the people was praying outside at the hour of the incense offering, the angel of the Lord appeared to him, standing at the right of the altar of incense. Zechariah was troubled by what he saw, and fear came upon him. But the angel said to him, "Do not be afraid, Zechariah, because your prayer has been heard. Your wife Elizabeth will bear you a son, and you shall name him John. (Luke 1:5–13)

The Wise Men Guided by the Star
By Paul Gustave Doré (1866)

"Where is the newborn king of the Jews? We saw his star at
its rising and have come to do him homage." (Matthew 2:2)

Induction: Body Scan

Start by finding a comfortable position. If you are sitting, have your feet grounded to the floor. If you are lying down, wriggle your feet and toes for comfort. Rest your arms and hands in a comfortable position, either on your lap or by your side, with hands open, closed, in prayer position, or whatever feels easiest for you. Now take three long, deep breaths, slowly breathing in and out from your lower belly area, in through your nose and out through your mouth. Gently close your eyes and begin to direct your attention to your body. Notice how it feels in this moment. Let yourself relax completely by releasing any areas of tension that you may sense, and feel the weight of your body simply loosening into total surrender. Begin to scan your body, starting from the top of your head and working your way slowly downward, moving throughout your head and into your neck, and now releasing tension throughout your shoulders and down into your arms and fingers. Feel the stress and tension floating right out of your body as you scan your entire frame. Imagine the anxiety and all negative energies exiting your body. Now move your attention down your diaphragm and into your stomach. Then move your attention throughout your back area, down to your hips and thigh area, letting all your muscles give up their hold. Now throughout your legs and right down into your toes.

Keep breathing, and as you exhale, let your body relax even more. Continue to take long, slow, deep breaths in and out. Notice the areas of your body that feel the most relaxed, and let this calm and relaxed feeling spread to any areas that may still feel some tension. Imagine your muscles melting into total relaxation, and now clear your mind, free your thoughts, and focus on my voice. You are going to be meeting with Mary and Elizabeth at the home of Zacharias.

Context

Envision that you are traveling back in time two thousand years ago to Israel in the Middle East. The Roman Empire has held control for sixty years, and King Herod the Great is tetrarch of Galilee in the province of Judea. Although he is Jewish, he is appointed by Rome to keep the Israelites in place. Times are tense, with the Jewish people being persecuted as they continue to pray for the coming of their long-prophesied messiah.

At that time, there was a priest named Zechariah of the priestly division of Abijah. His wife, Elizabeth, was from the daughters of Aaron. They had no children, as Elizabeth was past her child-bearing years. An angel of the Lord appeared to Zachariah and told him he would have a son and he would be great in the sight of the Lord. You are in the small village of Ein Karem, southwest of Jerusalem, a hilly region of Judah. You are in the home of Zechariah during the visitation of Mary. Mary has traveled from Nazareth to see her cousin Elizabeth.

> During those days Mary set out and traveled to the hill country in haste to a town of Judah, where she entered the house of Zechariah and greeted Elizabeth. When Elizabeth heard Mary's greeting, the infant leaped in her womb, and Elizabeth, filled with the holy Spirit, cried out in a loud voice and said, "Most blessed are you among women, and blessed is the fruit of your womb. And how does this happen to me, that the mother of my Lord should come to me? For at the moment the sound of your greeting reached my ears, the infant in my womb leaped for joy. Blessed are you who believed that what was spoken to you by the Lord would be fulfilled." (Luke 1:39–45)

Now ponder the virtue of the mystery, love of neighbor, the fruit of the visitation event, such an empathic experience for both Mary and Elizabeth, both bewildered by what has happened to them. It is a miraculous event that would eventually change the world. Consider the good news—the message that both of their sons would leave behind for all the world to live by of forgiveness and redemption, goodwill toward others, and no more sacrificial offerings, as Jesus would be the last sacrificial lamb of God, crucified for our salvation.

Today, you are there with Mary and Elizabeth in Ein Karem. You are a witness to this great event—the meeting of Mary and Elizabeth. Now ponder for a few moments on what this scene could bring to you today in your life!

(Take a long pause of three to five minutes.)

Reorientation

Now the scene begins to fade away, but his message lingers on in your heart and with all who honor him. Give thanks to God, and show gratitude for all that you are, the wondrous life and love you have around you. When you are ready to leave your peaceful place, you can begin to reawaken your body and mind. Feel your muscles reawakening as you take note of your surroundings and slowly return to the present. Wiggle your fingers and open and close your hands a few times. Wiggle your toes, and flex your ankles. Begin to move your arms and legs, and when you are ready, slowly reopen your eyes. Stretch if you desire to, feeling your body becoming fully awake. Now take a moment to sit quietly as you reawaken completely and further ponder the experience.

The Nativity of Our Lord Jesus Christ
Third Joyful Mystery
Fruit of the Mystery: Poverty—Love of the Poor

The nativity of Jesus in Bethlehem happened soon after Mary returned home from her visit to Elizabeth. In Christian theology, it marks the incarnation of Jesus as the second Adam, fulfilling the divine will of God, and correcting the damage of Adam's fall from grace. Again, the news was delivered by angelic creatures with the theme of poverty. God could have delivered his Son as a conqueror or nobleman among great riches, but instead he was sent to common people and was born in a stable, which would later reflect the message that Jesus delivered to the world.

> But you, Bethlehem-Ephrathah least among the clans of Judah, From you shall come forth for me one who is to be ruler in Israel; Whose origin is from of old, from ancient times. Therefore, the Lord will give them up, until the time when she who is to give birth has borne, Then the rest of his kindred shall return to the children of Israel. He shall take his place as shepherd by the strength of the Lord, by the majestic name of the Lord, his God; And they shall dwell securely, for now his greatness shall reach to the ends of the earth: he shall be peace. (Micah 5:1-3)

The Nativity
By Paul Gustave Doré (1866)

But you, Bethlehem-Ephrathah least among the clans of Judah, From you shall come forth for me one who is to be ruler in Israel; Whose origin is from of old, from ancient times. (Micah 5:1)

Induction: Body Scan

Start by finding a comfortable position. If you are sitting, have your feet grounded to the floor. If you are lying down, wriggle your feet and toes for comfort. Rest your arms and hands in a comfortable position, either on your lap or by your side, with hands open, closed, in prayer position, or whatever feels easiest for you. Now take three long, deep breaths, slowly breathing in and out from your lower belly area, in through your nose and out through your mouth. Gently close your eyes and begin to direct your attention to your body. Notice how it feels in this moment. Let yourself relax completely by releasing any areas of tension that you may sense, and feel the weight of your body simply loosening into total surrender. Begin to scan your body, starting from the top of your head and working your way slowly downward, moving throughout your head and into your neck, and now releasing tension throughout your shoulders and down into your arms and fingers. Feel the stress and tension floating right out of your body as you scan your entire frame. Imagine the anxiety and all negative energies exiting your body. Now move your attention down your diaphragm and into your stomach. Then move your attention throughout your back area, down to your hips and thigh area, letting all your muscles give up their hold. Now throughout your legs, right down into your toes.

Keep breathing, and as you exhale, let your body relax even more. Continue to take long, slow, deep breaths in and out. Notice the areas of your body that feel the most relaxed, and let this calm and relaxed feeling spread to any areas that may still feel some tension. Imagine your muscles melting into total relaxation, and now clear your mind, free your thoughts, and focus on my voice. You are going to be a witness to the birth of our Lord.

Context

Envision that you are traveling back in time two thousand years ago to Israel in the Middle East. The Roman Empire has held control for sixty years, and King Herod the Great is tetrarch of Galilee in the province of Judea. Although he is Jewish, he is appointed by Rome to keep the Israelites in place. Times are tense, with the Jewish people being persecuted as they continue to pray for the coming of their long-prophesied messiah.

You are in the small village of Bethlehem just outside of the city of Jerusalem. It is the nativity of our Savior, as written in the gospels of Luke and Matthew. Luke's account focuses on Mary, while Matthew's story takes place after the birth and centers on Joseph. In both narratives, however, angels are there singing a proclamation that a male boy has been born, a child that will become the Savior for all the world. Shepherds in the area flock to adore the infant child who descended from the house of David, the son of Mary and Joseph from Nazareth.

Imagine that you are there as dusk approaches. There is still some light out, but the sun is slowly setting below the horizon. Consider the details of your surroundings, the grass in the meadows, the trees and grounds around you, the stable, the flocks of sheep, the wondrous scene below. It is so peaceful watching the sky around you gradually darkening. The air around you is still and calm but begins cooling now against your face as the night slowly consumes the miraculous scene below. In the distance, you begin to hear faint singing beckoning from the skies.

> And suddenly there was a multitude of the heavenly host with the angel, praising God and saying: "Glory to God in the highest and on earth peace to those on whom his favor rests." When the angels went away from them to heaven, the shepherds said to one another, "Let us go, then, to Bethlehem to see this thing that has taken place, which the Lord has made known to us." (Luke 2:13–15)

You begin to see the first stars of the evening appear—first one star and then another and another. See how they twinkle, shining like tiny white crystals. As you look at the darkening sky, you notice one star greatly overshadowing all the rest. It is so huge and bright as it illuminates the whole evening scene below—the blessed star of Bethlehem.

The three magi who traveled from afar appear at the stable and place gifts before the manger: gifts of precious gold, frankincense, and myrrh. Western Christian tradition describes the three men as Balthasar, king of Arabia, Melchior, king of Persia, and Gaspar, the king of India. These men bow to pay homage to the child.

> When Jesus was born in Bethlehem of Judea, in the days of King Herod, behold, magi from the east arrived in

Jerusalem, saying, "Where is the newborn king of the Jews? We saw his star at its rising and have come to do him homage." When King Herod heard this, he was greatly troubled, and all Jerusalem with him. Assembling all the chief priests and the scribes of the people, he inquired of them where the Messiah was to be born. They said to him, "In Bethlehem of Judea, for thus it has been written through the prophet: And you, Bethlehem, land of Judah are by no means least among the rulers of Judah; since from you shall come a ruler, who is to shepherd my people Israel.'" (Matthew 2:1–6)

Now ponder the virtue of the mystery, poverty, the fruit of the nativity scene, such a humble yet miraculous event that would eventually change the world. Consider the good news that this child eventually leaves behind for all of us to live by—forgiveness and redemption, goodwill toward others, and no more sacrificial offerings, as he will be the last sacrificial lamb of God, crucified for our salvation. Now ponder for a few moments on what this scene could bring to you today in your life!

(Take a long pause of three to five minutes.)

Reorientation

Now the scene begins to fade away, but his message lingers on in your heart and with all who honor him. Give thanks to God and show gratitude for all that you are, the wondrous life and love that you have around you. When you are ready to leave your peaceful place, you can begin to reawaken your body and mind. Feel your muscles reawakening as you take note of your surroundings, and slowly return to the present. Wiggle your fingers, and open and close your hands a few times. Wiggle your toes and flex your ankles. Begin to move your arms and legs, and when you are ready, slowly reopen your eyes. Stretch if you desire to, feeling your body becoming fully awake. Now take a moment to sit quietly as you reawaken completely and further ponder the experience.

The Presentation of Our Lord
fourth Joyful Mystery
fruit of the Mystery: Obedience and Purity

The presentation of the baby Jesus at the temple celebrates the purification of Mary, an old Jewish rite from Mosaic law, later called Candlemas by the early Christians. This event mixes the purification ritual with the prophecy of Simien, which was fulfilled with his meeting of the Lord on the steps of the temple. The mystery has been celebrated since the fourth century as one of the oldest feasts in the Christian church.

> The Lord said to Moses: Tell the Israelites: When a woman has a child, giving birth to a boy, she shall be unclean for seven days, with the same uncleanness as during her menstrual period. On the eighth day, the flesh of the boy's foreskin shall be circumcised, and then she shall spend thirty-three days more in a state of blood purity; she shall not touch anything sacred nor enter the sanctuary till the days of her purification are fulfilled. If she gives birth to a girl, for fourteen days she shall be as unclean as during her menstrual period, after which she shall spend sixty-six days in a state of blood purity. When the days of her purification for a son or for a daughter are fulfilled, she shall bring to the priest at the entrance of the tent of meeting a yearling lamb for a burnt offering and a pigeon or a turtledove for a purification offering. (Leviticus 12:1–6)

The Flight into Egypt
By Paul Gustave Doré (1866)

When Israel was a child I loved him, out of Egypt I called my son. (Hosea 11:1)

Induction: Body Scan

Start by finding a comfortable position. If you are sitting, have your feet grounded to the floor. If you are lying down, wriggle your feet and toes for comfort. Rest your arms and hands in a comfortable position, either on your lap or by your side, with your hands open, closed, in prayer position, or whatever feels easiest for you. Now take three long, deep breaths, slowly breathing in and out from your lower belly area, in through your nose and out through your mouth. Gently close your eyes and begin to direct your attention to your body. Notice how it feels in this moment. Let yourself relax completely by releasing any areas of tension that you may sense, and feel the weight of your body simply loosening into total surrender. Begin to scan your body, starting from the top of your head working your way slowly downward, moving throughout your head and into your neck, now releasing tension throughout your shoulders and down into your arms and fingers. Feel the stress and tension floating right out of your body as you scan your entire frame. Imagine the anxiety and all negative energies exiting your body. Now move your attention down your diaphragm and into your stomach. Then move your attention throughout your back area, down to your hips and thigh area, letting all your muscles give up their hold and now throughout your legs, right down into your toes.

Keep breathing, and as you exhale, let your body relax even more. Continue to take long, slow, deep breaths in and out. Notice the areas of your body that feel the most relaxed, and let this calm and relaxed feeling spread to any areas that may still feel some tension. Imagine your muscles melting into total relaxation, and now clear your mind, free your thoughts, and focus on my voice. You are going to be a witness at the presentation of our Lord at the temple.

Context

Envision that you are traveling back in time two thousand years ago to Israel in the Middle East. The Roman Empire has held control for sixty years, and King Herod the Great is tetrarch of Galilee in the province of Judea. Although he is Jewish, he is appointed by Rome to keep the Israelites in place. Times are tense, with the Jewish people being persecuted as they continue to pray for the coming of their long-prophesied messiah.

You are at the steps of the second temple in the Old City. The second temple was built by Cyrus the Great after the Israelites returned from the Babylonian exile. Nebuchadnezzar destroyed the first temple built by Solomon, when he enforced the exile. Jewish law indicates that this event should take place forty days after birth for a male child, and hence today many celebrate the presentation forty days after Christmas.

The gospel of Luke tells the story of Simeon, who had been promised that "he should not see death before he had seen the Lord's Christ." Simeon then uttered the prayer that would become known as the *Nunc Dimittis*, or Canticle of Simeon, which prophesied the redemption of the world by Jesus:

> Now there was a man in Jerusalem whose name was Simeon. This man was righteous and devout, awaiting the consolation of Israel, and the holy Spirit was upon him. It had been revealed to him by the holy Spirit that he should not see death before he had seen the Messiah of the Lord. He came in the Spirit into the temple; and when the parents brought in the child Jesus to perform the custom of the law in regard to him, he took him into his arms and blessed God, saying: "Now, Master, you may let your servant go in peace, according to your word, for my eyes have seen your salvation, which you prepared in sight of all the peoples, a light for revelation to the Gentiles, and glory for your people Israel." (Luke 2:25-32)

Imagine that you are there on the steps of the temple that morning, the sun is shining directly overhead, and you watch as Joseph and Mary enter the building with the baby Jesus. The presentation marks the end of the Epiphany season. The Jewish temple, traditionally a very sacred place for the Israelites, stands high on the Temple Mount.

Now ponder the virtues of the mystery, obedience, and purity, the fruits of the presentation, such a gift of faith, a phenomenon that would begin Jesus's public ministry. The Holy Spirit descends upon Jesus, and he is sent into the desert for forty days of temptation by the devil. Consider the good news that this happening eventually leaves behind for all of us to live by, repentance, redemption, and salvation. Consider for a few moments what this scene could bring to you today in your life!

(Take a long pause of three to five minutes.)

Reorientation

Now the scene begins to fade away, but His message lingers on in your heart and with all who honor Him. Give thanks to God, and show gratitude for all that you are, the wondrous life and love you have around you. When you are ready to leave your peaceful place, you can begin to reawaken your body and mind. Feel your muscles reawakening as you take note of your surroundings and slowly return to the present. Wiggle your fingers, and open and close your hands a few times. Wiggle your toes and flex your ankles. Begin to move your arms and legs, and when you are ready, slowly reopen your eyes. Stretch if you desire to, feeling your body becoming fully awake. Now take a moment to sit quietly as you reawaken completely and further ponder the experience.

Finding Jesus in the Temple
Fifth Joyful Mystery
Fruit of the Mystery: Joy of Finding Jesus, True Wisdom and Conversion

The finding of Jesus in the temple, sometimes called Christ among the doctors, or the disputation, was the only event of the later childhood of Jesus mentioned in only one of the four gospels. Luke's gospel tells the story about a pilgrimage to Jerusalem when Jesus was twelve years old. It was discovered on the journey home that he was missing from the caravan. After three days of searching, Mary and Joseph found him in the temple in discourse with the elder Jewish priests. He defended himself to his parents by saying that they should have known where he would be: in his Father's house. This three-day void theme would later resurface with the resurrection in the passion story.

> Each year his parents went to Jerusalem for the feast of Passover, and when he was twelve years old, they went up according to festival custom. After they had completed its days, as they were returning, the boy Jesus remained behind in Jerusalem, but his parents did not know it. Thinking that he was in the caravan, they journeyed for a day and looked for him among their relatives and acquaintances, but not finding him, they returned to Jerusalem to look for him. After three days they found him in the temple, sitting in the midst of the teachers, listening to them and asking them questions, and all who heard him were astounded at his understanding and his answers. (Luke 2:41–47)

Jesus with the Doctors
By Paul Gustave Doré (1866)

Jesus answered them and said, "My teaching is not my own but is from the one who sent me." (John 7:16)

Induction: Body Scan

Start by finding a comfortable position. If you are sitting, have your feet grounded to the floor. If you are lying down, wriggle your feet and toes for comfort. Rest your arms and hands in a comfortable position, either on your lap or by your side, with hands open, closed, in prayer position, or whatever feels easiest for you. Now take three long, deep breaths, slowly breathing in and out from your lower belly area, in through your nose and out through your mouth. Gently close your eyes, and begin to direct your attention to your body and notice how it feels in this moment. Let yourself relax completely by releasing any areas of tension that you may sense, and feel the weight of your body simply loosening into total surrender. Begin to scan your body, starting from the top of your head and working your way slowly downward, moving throughout your head and into your neck, and now releasing tension throughout your shoulders and down into your arms and fingers. Feel the stress and tension floating right out of your body as you scan your entire frame. Imagine the anxiety and all negative energies exiting your body. Now move your attention down your diaphragm and into your stomach. Then move your attention throughout your back area, down to your hips and thigh area, letting all your muscles give up their hold. Now throughout your legs, right down into your toes.

Keep breathing, and as you exhale, let your body relax even more. Continue to take long, slow, deep breaths in and out. Notice the areas of your body that feel the most relaxed, and let this calm and relaxed feeling spread to any areas that may still feel some tension. Imagine your muscles melting into total relaxation, and now clear your mind, free your thoughts, and focus on my voice. You are going to be meeting with Jesus as a child in the temple.

Context

Envision that you are traveling back in time two thousand years ago to Israel in the Middle East. The Roman Empire has held control for sixty years, and King Herod the Great is tetrarch of Galilee in the province of Judea. Although he is Jewish, he is appointed by Rome to keep the Israelites in place. Times are tense, with the Jewish people being persecuted as they continue to pray for the coming of their long-prophesied messiah.

You are at the steps of the second temple in the Old City. The second temple was built by Cyrus the Great after the Israelites returned from the Babylonian exile. Nebuchadnezzar destroyed the first temple built by Solomon, when he enforced the exile.

Now ponder the virtues of the mystery, wisdom, and the joy of finding Jesus, the fruits of the finding of Jesus, such a humble, yet miraculous event that would eventually change the world. Consider the good news that this child eventually leaves behind for all of us to live by—forgiveness and redemption, good will toward others, and no more burnt offerings, as He will be the last sacrificial lamb of God, crucified for our salvation.

> When his parents saw him, they were astonished, and his mother said to him, "Son, why have you done this to us? Your father and I have been looking for you with great anxiety." And he said to them, "Why were you looking for me? Did you not know that I must be in my Father's house?" (Luke 2:48–49)

It is the week of the Passover celebration, and the streets are bustling. As you enter the temple, you hear voices of the rabbis and scribes pondering and debating the Jewish laws and customs. You notice there is a young boy there in the midst of all the elders. He is reciting scripture, and the surrounding rabbis are amazed. Now Mary and Joseph enter the temple in search of their son, and you direct them to where the boy is. You are a witness to this reunion of the holy family. Now ponder for a few moments on what this scene could bring to you today in your life!

(Take a long pause of three to five minutes.)

Reorientation

Now the scene begins to fade away, but His message lingers on in your heart and with all who honor Him. Give thanks to God, and show gratitude for all that you are, the wondrous life and love that you have around you. When you are ready to leave your peaceful place, you can begin to reawaken your body and mind. Feel your muscles reawakening as you take note of your surroundings and slowly return to the present. Wiggle your fingers, and open and close your hands a few times. Wiggle your toes, and flex your ankles. Begin to move your arms and legs, and when you are ready, slowly reopen your eyes. Stretch if you desire to, feeling your body becoming fully awake. Now take a moment to sit quietly as you reawaken completely and further ponder the experience.

4

The Sorrowful Mysteries

Secret Garden Induction Scripts
Theme: Redemption and Forgiveness

The Agony of Jesus in the Garden
The Scourging at the Pillar
Jesus is Crowned with Thorns
Jesus Carries the Cross
The Crucifixion of our Lord

The sorrowful mysteries, rightly named, reflect on fruits such as redemption, forgiveness, atonement, and reparation between God and humanity. But it is most sorrowful because it includes the suffering and crucifixion of Christ. This event symbolizes Christ as the last sacrificial lamb, as one of His messages was to stop the sacrificing of animals to God. The focus on these events are on Jesus and his suffering, and through that suffering all human sin is restored to grace.

Psalm 143
A Prayer in Distress

A psalm of David.
Lord, hear my prayer;
in your faithfulness listen to my pleading;
answer me in your righteousness.
Do not enter into judgment with your servant;
before you no one can be just.
The enemy has pursued my soul;
he has crushed my life to the ground.
He has made me dwell in darkness
like those long dead.
My spirit is faint within me;
my heart despairs.
I remember the days of old;
I ponder all your deeds;
the works of your hands I recall.
I stretch out my hands toward you,
my soul to you like a parched land.
Hasten to answer me, Lord;
for my spirit fails me.
Do not hide your face from me,
lest I become like those descending to the pit.
In the morning let me hear of your mercy,
for in you I trust.
Show me the path I should walk,
for I entrust my life to you.
Rescue me, Lord, from my foes,
for I seek refuge in you.
Teach me to do your will,
for you are my God.
May your kind spirit guide me
on ground that is level.

For your name's sake, Lord, give me life;
in your righteousness lead my soul out of distress.
In your mercy put an end to my foes;
all those who are oppressing my soul,
for I am your servant.

Jesus and his disciples went on to the villages around
Caesarea Philippi. On the way he asked them, "Who do
people say I am?" They replied, "Some say John the Baptist;
others say Elijah; and still others, one of the prophets."
"But what about you?" he asked. "Who do you say I am?"
Peter answered, "You are the Messiah." Jesus warned them
not to tell anyone about him. (Mark 8:27–30)

The Agony of Jesus in the Garden
First Sorrowful Mystery
Fruit of the Mystery: Sorrow for Sin

In Roman Catholic tradition, the agony in the garden is both the first sorrowful mystery of the rosary and the first station of the scriptural way of the cross. In the garden of Gethsemane Jesus sweat blood while praying that he be released from this burden, knowing what lay ahead for him. In excruciating anguish, he was comforted by an angel of mercy, sent by God. According to the gospels, Christ was arrested at the Gethsemane site where he went to pray with three of his apostles after his last supper with the twelve. This event is known to have been on Thursday evening of the week of the Passover celebration in Jerusalem. With the Jewish Sanhedrin and High Priest Caliphas leading the persecution, the governor, Pontius Pilate, was coerced into sentencing Jesus to a scourging and later, a crucifixion. One of his apostles, Judas, was named to have contacted the temple guards as to his whereabouts that evening.

> He took with him Peter, James, and John, and began to be troubled and distressed. Then he said to them, "My soul is sorrowful even to death. Remain here and keep watch." He advanced a little and fell to the ground and prayed that if it were possible the hour might pass by him; he said, "Abba, Father, all things are possible to you. Take this cup away from me, but not what I will but what you will." When he returned he found them asleep. He said to Peter, "Simon, are you asleep? Could you not keep watch for one hour? Watch and pray that you may not undergo the test. The spirit is willing but the flesh is weak." Withdrawing again, he prayed, saying the same thing. Then he returned once more and found them asleep, for they could not keep their eyes open and did not know what to answer him. (Mark 14:33–40)

The Agony in the Garden
By Paul Gustave Doré (1866)

Watch and pray that you may not undergo the test. The
spirit is willing, but the flesh is weak. (Matthew 26:41)

Induction: Secret Garden

Start by finding a comfortable position. If you are sitting, have your feet grounded to the floor. If you are lying down, wriggle your feet and toes for comfort. Rest your arms and hands in a comfortable position, either on your lap or by your side, with hands open, closed, in prayer position, or whatever feels easiest for you. Now take three long, deep breaths, slowly breathing in and out from your lower belly area, in through your nose, out through your mouth. Gently begin to close your eyes and let yourself soften completely by releasing areas of tension and any negative energies. Imagine that all the stress you harbor is leaving your body.

Imagine now that you are standing on a balcony overlooking a beautiful garden. It's a lovely, warm summer evening, and the air is filled with the fragrant smell of sweet-scented flowers. Part of the garden is hidden, and you really want to go down there. Ten steps lead down from the balcony into the garden, and you begin to walk down the steps, counting with me in your mind as you go down. Ten, the day is perfect. Nine, you seem to just float down the stairs. Eight, the flowers smell so fresh. Seven, the air is so clean. Six, you are so happy in that garden. Five, as you go down the stairs, four, you seem to be floating. Three, down, down, two, down, one.

Now you're standing at the bottom of the steps, and you see a little white stone pathway that winds through a wooden archway into a private garden. Flowers cling to the entrance, and there are weeping willows on either side. Birds are singing in the trees, and there's a soft, gentle breeze. You can feel it on your skin. Walking through the garden, you feel peace and the calmness it brings to you. Let this calm and relaxed feeling flow through any areas of your body that may still feel some tension. Your muscles melt into total relaxation, and now clear your mind, free your thoughts, and focus on my voice. You are going to be meeting with Jesus in another garden, the garden of Gethsemane.

Context

Envision that you are traveling back in time two thousand years. You are in the city of Jerusalem during the time of Jesus. It is the Passover celebration week. The Romans are in control of the area, and Pontius Pilate is the current prefect to Rome. Herod Antipas is tetrarch of Galilee in the province of Judea, and although he is Jewish, he is appointed by Rome to

keep the Israelites in place. The high priest of the Jewish temple is Calipas, and he desperately needs to keep peace and order among the Jews. Rome has made it clear that if problems arise, worship in the temple will be halted.

It is Thursday during the Passover week celebration, and Jesus has just eaten his last supper with his apostles in the upper room. According to all four gospels, directly after the supper, Jesus took a walk to pray. Both Matthew and Mark identify this place of prayer as Gethsemane. The agony in the garden is the event that begins the passion of Christ, where Jesus was overcome with fear and grief for what he was about to face.

> And to strengthen him an angel from heaven appeared to
> him. He was in such agony and he prayed so fervently that
> his sweat became like drops of blood falling on the ground.
> When he rose from prayer and returned to his disciples, he
> found them sleeping from grief. (Luke 22:43–45)

Ponder the virtue of sorrow for sin, the fruit of Jesus's agony in the garden. Consider what Jesus is going through, how betrayed he must feel knowing that his closest companions will betray him before the night is over. Forgiveness is a gift of God and a practice for all of us to live by—forgiveness and redemption, as he knew that night that he would be the last sacrificial lamb of God, crucified for our salvation.

Now imagine that you are there in the garden as dusk approaches. The air around you is still and calm but begins cooling now against your face, as the night slowly consumes the scene. In the distance, you begin to hear soldiers coming. There is still some light out, but the sun is slowly setting below the horizon. Consider the details of your surroundings, the grass in the meadows, the grounds around you, and the olive trees in the garden. Perhaps you are sitting under one. Now place yourself in the scene. Tonight you are a witness to the most profound night in history, an event that would eventually change the world.

As the soldiers get closer, Jesus motions to you as if he wants to talk with you. He is distraught with fear, but he takes your hand, looks into your eyes, and bows his head to whisper something to you, so you look away to put your ear near his voice. Now listen for a moment to what he is saying to you.

(Take a long pause of three to five minutes.)

Reorientation

Now the scene begins to fade away, but His message lingers on in your heart and with all who honor Him. Give thanks to God and show gratitude for all that you are, the wondrous life and love that you have around you. When you are ready to leave your peaceful place, you can begin to reawaken your body and mind. Feel your muscles reawakening as you take note of your surroundings and slowly return to the present. Wiggle your fingers, and open and close your hands a few times. Wiggle your toes, and flex your ankles. Begin to move your arms and legs, and when you are ready, slowly reopen your eyes. Stretch if you desire to, feeling your body becoming fully awake. Now take a moment to sit quietly as you reawaken completely and further ponder the experience.

The Scourging at the Pillar
Second Sorrowful Mystery
Fruit of the Mystery: Mortification

The flagellation of Christ, also known as Christ at the column, or the scourging at the pillar, is a scene often depicted from the passion week. After the flogging, according to three of the gospels (Matthew, Mark, John), a woven crown of thorns was placed on his head during the events leading to the crucifixion. It was one of many tactics used by Jesus's captors to cause him pain and to mock his claims of being the Son of God.

> So Pilate went back into the praetorium and summoned Jesus and said to him, "Are you the King of the Jews?" Jesus answered, "Do you say this on your own or have others told you about me?" Pilate answered, "I am not a Jew, am I? Your own nation and the chief priests handed you over to me. What have you done?" Jesus answered, "My kingdom does not belong to this world. If my kingdom did belong to this world, my attendants [would] be fighting to keep me from being handed over to the Jews. But as it is, my kingdom is not here." So Pilate said to him, "Then you are a king?" Jesus answered, "You say I am a king. For this I was born and for this I came into the world, to testify to the truth. Everyone who belongs to the truth listens to my voice." Pilate said to him, "What is truth?" When he had said this, he again went out to the Jews and said to them, "I find no guilt in him. (John 18:33–38)

Jesus Scourged
By Paul Gustave Doré (1866)

Then he released Barabbas to them, but after he had Jesus scourged, he handed him over to be crucified. (Matthew 27:26)

Induction: Secret Garden

Start by finding a comfortable position. If you are sitting, have your feet grounded to the floor. If you are lying down, wriggle your feet and toes for comfort. Rest your arms and hands in a comfortable position, either on your lap or by your side, with hands open, closed, in prayer position, or whatever feels easiest for you. Now take three long, deep breaths, slowly breathing in and out from your lower belly area, in through your nose, out through your mouth. Gently begin to close your eyes and let yourself soften completely by releasing areas of tension and any negative energies. Imagine that all the stress you harbor is leaving your body.

Imagine now that you are standing on a balcony overlooking a beautiful garden. It's a lovely, warm summer evening and the air is filled with the fragrant smell of sweet-scented flowers. Part of the garden is hidden, and you really want to go down there. Ten steps lead down from the balcony into the garden, and you begin to walk down the steps, counting with me in your mind as you go down. Ten, the day is perfect. Nine, you seem to just float down the stairs. Eight, the flowers smell so fresh. Seven, the air is so clean. Six, you are so happy in that garden. Five, as you go down the stairs, four, you seem to be floating, three, down, down, two, down, one.

Now you're standing at the bottom of the steps, and you see a little white stone pathway that winds through a wooden archway into a private garden. Flowers cling to the entrance, and there are weeping willows on either side. Birds are singing in the trees, and there's a soft, gentle breeze. You can feel it on your skin. Walking through the garden, you feel peace and the calmness it brings to you. Let this calm and relaxed feeling flow through any areas of your body that may still feel some tension. Your muscles melt into total relaxation, and now clear your mind, free your thoughts, and focus on my voice. You are going to be meeting with Jesus in the courtyard of Pontius Pilate.

Context

Envision that you are traveling back in time two thousand years. You are in the city of Jerusalem during the time of Jesus. It is the Passover celebration week. The Romans are in control of the area, and Pontius Pilate is the current prefect to Rome. Herod Antipas is tetrarch of Galilee in the province of Judea, and although he is Jewish, he is appointed by Rome to

keep the Israelites in place. The high priest of the Jewish temple is Calipas, and he desperately needs to keep peace and order among the Jews. Rome has made it clear that if problems arise, worship in the temple will be halted.

It is Thursday during the Passover week celebration, and Jesus has just eaten his last supper with his apostles in the upper room. The scourging at the pillar is an event that continues the passion of Christ. The meditation on this event will encourage you into deep sorrow for your own sins, as it is those sins and the sins of all people who ever lived that caused Jesus's agony. Mortification is the subjective experience of sanctification, the objective work of God between justification and glorification. It means the 'putting to death' of sin. Contrition is the emotion of remorse of your sins, and feeling true distress for offending God so much so that you never want to commit that sin again. It is a godly sorrow, which through God's grace initiates change in the way a person thinks or behaves. Worldly sorrow lacks repentance and results in further mental suffering and eventual spiritual death. Confronting your sins and showing penitence for them is the only route to mending relationships, including your relationship with God, and gaining true peace of mind. This kind of sorrow that God wants us to experience helps to keep us away from future sins and results in our salvation.

> Then Pilate took Jesus and had him scourged. And the soldiers wove a crown out of thorns and placed it on his head, and clothed him in a purple cloak, and they came to him and said, "Hail, King of the Jews!" And they struck him repeatedly. (John 19:1–3)

Now ponder the virtue of mortification, the fruit of the crowning of thorns. Consider what Jesus is going through, how betrayed he must feel knowing that his closest companions will betray him before the night is over. Forgiveness is a gift of God and a practice for all of us to live by— forgiveness and redemption, as he knew that night that he would be the last sacrificial lamb of God, crucified for our salvation. As the soldiers begin to move toward Jesus, he motions to you as if he wants to talk with you. He begins to take your hands softly into his and bows his head to whisper something to you, and so you look away to put your ear near his voice. Now listen for a moment to what he is saying to you.

Reorientation

Now the scene begins to fade away, but his message lingers on in your heart and with all who honor Him. Give thanks to God, and show gratitude for all that you are, the wondrous life and love that you have around you. When you are ready to leave your peaceful place, you can begin to reawaken your body and mind. Feel your muscles reawakening as you take note of your surroundings and slowly return to the present. Wiggle your fingers, and open and close your hands a few times. Wiggle your toes and flex your ankles. Begin to move your arms and legs, and when you are ready, slowly reopen your eyes. Stretch if you desire to, feeling your body becoming fully awake. Now take a moment to sit quietly as you reawaken completely and further ponder the experience.

Jesus Is Crowned with Thorns
Third Sorrowful Mystery
Fruit of the Mystery: Contempt of the World

After the flogging at the pillar, a crown of thorns was placed on Jesus's head, merely meant to inflict more pain. Jesus with his crown of thorns is a scene often depicted from the passion week. According to three of the gospels (Matthew, Mark, John), a woven crown of thorns was placed on his head during the events leading to the crucifixion. It was one of many tactics used by Jesus's captors to cause him pain and to mock his claims of being the Son of God.

> And the soldiers wove a crown out of thorns and placed it on his head, and clothed him in a purple cloak, and they came to him and said, "Hail, King of the Jews!" And they struck him repeatedly. Once more Pilate went out and said to them, "Look, I am bringing him out to you, so that you may know that I find no guilt in him." So Jesus came out, wearing the crown of thorns and the purple cloak. And he said to them, "Behold, the man!" When the chief priests and the guards saw him they cried out, "Crucify him, crucify him!" Pilate said to them, "Take him yourselves and crucify him. I find no guilt in him." (John 19:2–4)

The Crown of Thorns
By Paul Gustave Doré (1866)

Weaving a crown out of thorns, they placed it on his head,
and a reed in his right hand. And kneeling before him, they
mocked him, saying, "Hail, King of the Jews!" (Matthew
27:29)

Induction: Secret Garden

Start by finding a comfortable position. If you are sitting, have your feet grounded to the floor. If you are lying down, wriggle your feet and toes for comfort. Rest your arms and hands in a comfortable position, either on your lap or by your side, with hands open, closed, in prayer position, or whatever feels easiest for you. Now take three long, deep breaths, slowly breathing in and out from your lower belly area, in through your nose, out through your mouth. Gently begin to close your eyes and let yourself soften completely by releasing areas of tension and any negative energies. Imagine that all the stress you harbor is leaving your body.

Imagine now that you are standing on a balcony overlooking a beautiful garden. It's a lovely, warm summer evening, and the air is filled with the fragrant smell of sweet-scented flowers. Part of the garden is hidden, and you really want to go down there. Ten steps lead down from the balcony into the garden, and you begin to walk down the steps, counting with me in your mind as you go down. Ten, the day is perfect. Nine, you seem to just float down the stairs. Eight, the flowers smell so fresh. Seven, the air is so clean. Six, you are so happy in that garden. Five, as you go down the stairs, four, you seem to be floating, three, down, down, two, down, one.

Now you're standing at the bottom of the steps, and you see a little white stone pathway that winds through a wooden archway into a private garden. Flowers cling to the entrance, and there are weeping willows on either side. Birds are singing in the trees, and there's a soft, gentle breeze. You can feel it on your skin. Walking through the garden you feel peace and the calmness it brings to you. Let this calm and relaxed feeling flow through any areas of your body that may still feel some tension. Your muscles melt into total relaxation, and now clear your mind, free your thoughts, and focus on my voice. You are going to be meeting with Jesus in the courtyard of Pontius Pilate.

Context

Envision that you are traveling back in time two thousand years. You are in the city of Jerusalem during the time of Jesus. It is the Passover celebration week. The Romans are in control of the area, and Pontius Pilate is the current prefect to Rome. Herod Antipas is tetrarch of Galilee in the province of Judea, and although he is Jewish, he is appointed by Rome to keep the Israelites in place. The high priest of the Jewish temple is Calipas, and he desperately needs to keep peace and order among the Jews. Rome has made it clear that if problems arise, worship in the temple will be halted.

It is late Thursday night of Passover week, and Jesus has broken bread with his twelve apostles, warning them that he would be betrayed. He later went to the garden of Gethsemane to pray, taken by the temple guards, brought to the Sanhedrin for questioning, and then sentenced by Pontius Pilate for crucifixion.

> The soldiers led him away inside the palace, that is, the praetorium, and assembled the whole cohort. They clothed him in purple and, weaving a crown of thorns, placed it on him. They began to salute him with, "Hail, King of the Jews!" and kept striking his head with a reed and spitting upon him. They knelt before him in homage. And when they had mocked him, they stripped him of the purple cloak, dressed him in his own clothes, and led him out to crucify him. (Mark 15:16–20)

Now imagine that you are there in the courtyard where Jesus was scourged and crowned. The air around you is still and calm but begins cooling now against your face, as the night slowly consumes the scene. There is still darkness, with the sun just rising. Now place yourself in the scene. Tonight you are a witness to the most profound night in history, an event that would eventually change the world, and for a moment Jesus's eyes lock onto yours.

Now ponder the virtue of contempt of the world, the fruit of the crowning of thorns. Consider what Jesus is going through, how betrayed he must feel knowing that one of his closest companions turned on him. Forgiveness is a gift of God and a practice for all of us to live by—forgiveness and redemption, as He knew that night that he would be the last sacrificial lamb of God, crucified for our salvation.

The meditation on this sad event will encourage you when your own life begins to unravel and takes you to a place you don't want to be. It reminds you to hold tight to your patience and faith. A light awaits, and he has a plan for you. Now ponder for a few moments on what this scene could bring to you today in your life!

(Take a long pause of three to five minutes.)

Reorientation

Now the scene begins to fade away, but His message lingers on in your heart and with all who honor Him. Give thanks to God and show gratitude for all that you are, the wondrous life and love that you have around you. When you are ready to leave your peaceful place, you can begin to reawaken your body and mind. Feel your muscles reawakening as you take note of your surroundings, and slowly return to the present. Wiggle your fingers and open and close your hands a few times. Wiggle your toes and flex your ankles. Begin to move your arms and legs, and when you are ready, slowly reopen your eyes. Stretch if you desire to, feeling your body becoming fully awake. Now take a moment to sit quietly as you reawaken completely and further ponder the experience.

Jesus Carries the Cross
Fourth Sorrowful Mystery
Fruit of the Mystery: Patience

General consensus is that the crucifixion was on a Friday, on or near the Jewish Passover, between the years of AD 26 and 36, more closely estimated at AD 30 to 33. Christ's crucifixion journey has many names: carrying of the cross, procession to Calvary, road to Calvary, and way of the cross. The name of the location outside of the city walls of Jerusalem where the cross was placed is called Calvary or Golgotha, Latin for place of the skull. The route taken to that location traditionally has been called the Via Dolorosa, Latin for way of grief or way of suffering. The specific path of this route has been debated, although the general location is known and venerated today.

> So Pilate said to him, "Do you not speak to me? Do you not know that I have power to release you and I have power to crucify you?" Jesus answered him, "You would have no power over me if it had not been given to you from above. Pilate tried to release him; but the Jews cried out, "If you release him, you are not a Friend of Caesar. Everyone who makes himself a king opposes Caesar." When Pilate heard these words he brought Jesus out and seated him on the judge's bench in the place called Stone Pavement, in Hebrew, Gabbatha. It was preparation day for Passover, and it was about noon. And he said to the Jews, "Behold, your king!" They cried out, "Take him away, take him away! Crucify him!" Pilate said to them, "Shall I crucify your king?" The chief priests answered, "We have no king but Caesar." Then he handed him over to them to be crucified. So they took Jesus, and carrying the cross himself he went out to what is called the Place of the Skull, in Hebrew, Golgotha. (John 19:10–17)

Jesus Falling Beneath the Cross
By Paul Gustave Doré (1866)

Then Jesus said to his disciples, "Whoever wishes to come after me must deny himself, take up his cross, and follow me." (Matthew 16:24)

Induction: Secret Garden

Start by finding a comfortable position. If you are sitting, have your feet grounded to the floor. If you are lying down, wriggle your feet and toes for comfort. Rest your arms and hands in a comfortable position, either on your lap or by your side, with hands open, closed, in prayer position, or whatever feels easiest for you. Now take three long, deep breaths, slowly breathing in and out from your lower belly area, in through your nose, out through your mouth. Gently begin to close your eyes, and let yourself soften completely by releasing areas of tension and any negative energies. Imagine that all the stress you harbor is leaving your body.

Imagine now that you are standing on a balcony overlooking a beautiful garden. It's a lovely, warm summer evening, and the air is filled with the fragrant smell of sweet-scented flowers. Part of the garden is hidden, and you really want to go down there. Ten steps lead down from the balcony into the garden, and you begin to walk down the steps, counting with me in your mind as you go down. Ten, the day is perfect. Nine, you seem to just float down the stairs. Eight, the flowers smell so fresh. Seven, the air is so clean. Six, you are so happy in that garden. Five, as you go down the stairs, four, you seem to be floating, three, down, down, two, down, one.

Now you're standing at the bottom of the steps, and you see a little white stone pathway that winds through a wooden archway into a private garden. Flowers cling to the entrance, and there are weeping willows on either side. Birds are singing in the trees, and there's a soft, gentle breeze. You can feel it on your skin. Walking through the garden, you feel peace and the calmness it brings to you. Let this calm and relaxed feeling flow through any areas of your body that may still feel some tension. Your muscles melt into total relaxation, and now clear your mind, free your thoughts, and focus on my voice. You are going to be meeting with Jesus on the road to Calvary.

Context

Envision that you are traveling back in time two thousand years. You are in the city of Jerusalem during the time of Jesus. It is the Passover celebration week. The Romans are in control of the area, and Pontius Pilate is the current prefect to Rome. Herod Antipas is tetrarch of Galilee in the province of Judea, and although he is Jewish, he is appointed by Rome to keep the Israelites in place. The high priest of the Jewish temple is Calipas, and he desperately needs to keep peace and order among the Jews. Rome has made it clear that if problems arise, worship in the temple will be halted.

It is early Friday morning of Passover week. Jesus had been brought to the Sanhedrin for questioning through the night, then to Pilate for a crucifixion sentencing, then scourged, and crowned with thorns and given his cross to carry.

Now imagine you are a bystander on the street where Jesus carried his cross to Golgotha on the hill, called the Via Dolorosa today, translated as the way of suffering. Consider the details of your surroundings, the cobblestone city street in Old Jerusalem. Today you are a witness to the most profound day in history, an event that would eventually change the world. John tells us that Jesus carried his own cross, but the three Synoptic gospels state that a Cyrenian named Simon was ordered by the soldiers to help him.

> As they led him away they took hold of a certain Simon, a Cyrenian, who was coming in from the country; and after laying the cross on him, they made him carry it behind Jesus. A large crowd of people followed Jesus, including many women who mourned and lamented him. (Luke 23:26–27)

The meditation on this sad event will encourage you when your own life begins to unravel into a dark place that you don't want to be. It reminds you to hold tight to your patience and faith in the Lord, that a light awaits, and he has a plan for you.

Consider the virtue of patience, the fruit of the carrying of the cross. Consider what Jesus is going through, how betrayed he must feel knowing that his closest companions will betray him before the night is over. Forgiveness is a gift of God and a practice for all of us to live by—forgiveness and redemption, as He knew that night that he would be the last sacrificial lamb of God, crucified for our salvation.

Now Jesus falls with the wooden cross right in front of you. He turns and looks directly into your eyes. He motions to you, and you wipe his brow and get closer to him. He reaches out and whispers something in your ear. Now sit and ponder the meaning of his words.

(Take a long pause of three to five minutes.)

Reorientation

Now the scene begins to fade away, but his message lingers on in your heart and with all who honor him. Give thanks to God, and show gratitude for all that you are, the wondrous life and love that you have around you. When you are ready to leave your peaceful place, you can begin to reawaken your body and mind. Feel your muscles reawakening as you take note of your surroundings, and slowly return to the present. Wiggle your fingers, and open and close your hands a few times. Wiggle your toes and flex your ankles. Begin to move your arms and legs, and when you are ready, slowly reopen your eyes. Stretch if you desire to, feeling your body becoming fully awake. Now take a moment to sit quietly as you reawaken completely and further ponder the experience.

The Crucifixion of our Lord
Fifth Sorrowful Mystery
Fruit of the Mystery: Salvation

The events of the last week of Jesus's life are known as the passion of Christ and characterized by his suffering and redemptive death, which is central to Christian theology concerning the doctrines of salvation and atonement. The coming of the Messiah was prophesied throughout the Old Testament.

> And I will pour upon the house of David, and upon the inhabitants of Jerusalem, the spirit of grace and of supplication; and they shall look unto Me because they have thrust him through; and they shall mourn for him, as one mourneth for his only son, and shall be in bitterness for him, as one that is in bitterness for his first-born. (Zechariah 12:10)

Jesus's last words from the cross:

> Father, forgive them, for they do not know what they do. (Luke 23:34)

> Truly, I say to you, today you will be with me in paradise. (Luke 23:43)

> Woman, behold your son. Son, behold your mother. (John 19:26–27)

> My God, My God, why have you forsaken me? (Matthew 27:46, Mark 15:34)

> I thirst. (John 19:28)

> It is finished. (John 19:30)

Father, into your hands I commend my spirit. (Luke 23:46)

The people stood by and watched; the rulers, meanwhile, sneered at him and said, "He saved others, let him save himself if he is the chosen one, the Messiah of God." Even the soldiers jeered at him. As they approached to offer him wine they called out, "If you are King of the Jews, save yourself." Above him there was an inscription that read, "This is the King of the Jews." (Luke 23:35–38)

The Erection of the Cross
By Paul Gustave Doré (1866)

When the centurion who stood facing him saw how he breathed his last he said, "Truly this man was the Son of God!" (Mark 15:39)

Induction: Secret Garden

Start by finding a comfortable position. If you are sitting, have your feet grounded to the floor. If you are lying down, wriggle your feet and toes for comfort. Rest your arms and hands in a comfortable position, either on your lap or by your side, with hands open, closed, in prayer position, or whatever feels easiest for you. Now take three long, deep breaths, slowly breathing in and out from your lower belly area, in through your nose, out through your mouth. Gently begin to close your eyes, and let yourself soften completely by releasing areas of tension and any negative energies. Imagine that all the stress you harbor is leaving your body.

Imagine now that you are standing on a balcony overlooking a beautiful garden. It's a lovely, warm summer evening, and the air is filled with the fragrant smell of sweet-scented flowers. Part of the garden is hidden, and you really want to go down there. Ten steps lead down from the balcony into the garden, and you begin to walk down the steps, counting with me in your mind as you go down. Ten, the day is perfect. Nine, you seem to just float down the stairs. Eight, the flowers smell so fresh. Seven, the air is so clean. Six, you are so happy in that garden. Five, as you go down the stairs, four, you seem to be floating, three, down, down, two, down, one.

Now you're standing at the bottom of the steps, and you see a little white stone pathway that winds through a wooden archway into a private garden. Flowers cling to the entrance, and there are weeping willows on either side. Birds are singing in the trees, and there's a soft, gentle breeze. You can feel it on your skin. Walking through the garden, you feel peace and the calmness it brings to you. Let this calm and relaxed feeling flow through any areas of your body that may still feel some tension. Your muscles melt into total relaxation, and now clear your mind, free your thoughts, and focus on my voice. You are going to be meeting with Jesus at Calvary Hill, Golgotha, the place of the skull.

Context

Envision that you are traveling back in time two thousand years. You are in the city of Jerusalem during the time of Jesus. It is the Passover celebration week. The Romans are in control of the area, and Pontius Pilate is the current prefect to Rome. Herod Antipas is tetrarch of Galilee in the province of Judea, and although he is Jewish, he is appointed by Rome to

keep the Israelites in place. The high priest of the Jewish temple is Calipas, and he desperately needs to keep peace and order among the Jews. Rome has made it clear that if problems arise, worship in the temple will be halted.

It is early Friday morning of Passover week. Jesus had been brought to the Sanhedrin for questioning through the night, then to Pilate for a crucifixion sentencing, then scourged, crowned with thorns, and given his cross to carry to Golgotha on the hill.

Now imagine you are at the foot of the cross with his mother Mary, Mary Magdalene, and James during the crucifixion. Today you are a witness to the most profound day in history, an event that would eventually change the world. Those passing by the cross, including the chief priests, mocked and reviled Jesus as he hung there, and darkness came over the land until 3:00 that afternoon when he died.

> And at three o'clock Jesus cried out in a loud voice, "Eloi, Eloi, lema sabachthani?" which is translated, "My God, my God, why have you forsaken me?" Some of the bystanders who heard it said, "Look, he is calling Elijah." One of them ran, soaked a sponge with wine, put it on a reed, and gave it to him to drink, saying, "Wait, let us see if Elijah comes to take him down." Jesus gave a loud cry and breathed his last. The veil of the sanctuary was torn in two from top to bottom. (Mark 15:34–38)

Consider the virtue of salvation, the fruit of the crucifixion. Consider what Jesus is going through, how alone and betrayed he must have felt, persecuted by his own people. Forgiveness is a gift of God and a practice for all of us to live by—forgiveness and redemption, as He knew that night that he would be the last sacrificial lamb of God, crucified for our salvation.

Now Jesus breathes his last breath on the cross in front of you. The meditation on this sad event will encourage you when your own life begins to unravel and takes you to a place you don't want to be. It reminds you to hold tight to your patience and faith. A light awaits, and he has a plan for you. Now ponder for a few moments on what this scene could bring to you today in your life!

(Take a long pause of three to five minutes.)

Reorientation

Now the scene begins to fade away, but his message lingers on in your heart and with all who honor him. Give thanks to God, and show gratitude for all that you are, the wondrous life and love that you have around you. When you are ready to leave your peaceful place, you can begin to reawaken your body and mind. Feel your muscles reawakening as you take note of your surroundings, and slowly return to the present. Wiggle your fingers, and open and close your hands a few times. Wiggle your toes, and flex your ankles. Begin to move your arms and legs, and when you are ready, slowly reopen your eyes. Stretch if you desire to, feeling your body becoming fully awake. Now take a moment to sit quietly as you reawaken completely and further ponder the experience.

5

The Glorious Mysteries

✝

White Light Induction Scripts
Theme: Faith and Heaven

The Resurrection of Jesus Christ
The Ascension of Jesus to Heaven
The Descent of the Holy Spirit
The Assumption of Mary into Heaven
Mary is crowned as Queen of Heaven and Earth

The glorious mysteries, rightly named, reflect on fruits such faith, perseverance, and the fruits of the passion, resulting in the glory of God as he promised. Christ did not leave us orphaned. He left us with the Holy Spirit and the Catholic Church to preserve the message that he taught during his three-year public ministry. The focus on these events are shared by both Jesus and Mary, which especially portrays their triumph over evil.

Psalm 70
Prayer for Divine Help

For the leader; of David. For remembrance.
Graciously rescue me, God!
Come quickly to help me, Lord!
Let those who seek my life
be confused and put to shame.
Let those who desire my ruin
turn back in disgrace.
Let those who say "Aha!"
turn back in their shame.
But may all who seek you
rejoice and be glad in you,
Those who long for your help
always say, "God be glorified!"
I am miserable and poor.
God, come to me quickly!
You are my help and deliverer.
Lord, do not delay!

Psalm 112
The Blessings of the Just

Hallelujah!
Blessed the man who fears the Lord,
who greatly delights in his commands.
His descendants shall be mighty in the land,
a generation of the upright will be blessed.
Wealth and riches shall be in his house;
his righteousness shall endure forever.
Light shines through the darkness for the upright;
gracious, compassionate, and righteous.
It is good for the man gracious in lending,
who conducts his affairs with justice.
For he shall never be shaken;
the righteous shall be remembered forever.
He shall not fear an ill report;
his heart is steadfast, trusting the Lord.
His heart is tranquil, without fear,
till at last he looks down on his foes.
Lavishly he gives to the poor;
his righteousness shall endure forever;
his horn shall be exalted in honor.
The wicked sees and is angry;
gnashes his teeth and wastes away;
the desire of the wicked come to nothing.

The Resurrection of Jesus Christ
First Glorious Mystery
The Resurrection. Fruit of the Mystery: Faith

The resurrection of Jesus is the Christian belief that Jesus rose from the dead on the third day. According to the gospels, Jesus was anointed and buried in a tomb owned by Joseph of Arimathea, a member of the Sanhedrin, but also a follower of Christ. Jesus reappeared to many people over the forty days after he rose and walked the earth and before he ascended into heaven. Christians celebrate the resurrection on Easter Sunday, which generally coincides with the Jewish Passover. The risen Christ remains a central theme of the mystery of faith. This concept of redemption through faith in God leading to salvation and entry into heaven was Paul's main argument that salvation comes to all people, Jews and Gentiles equally, through faith in Christ, apart from following Jewish law. Those who accept and have faith in Christ's death are put into a right standing with God, something that cannot be completed by keeping Jewish law alone. Jewish law can only condemn and cannot forgive or offer salvation.

> For I handed on to you as of first importance what I also received: that Christ died for our sins in accordance with the scriptures; that he was buried; that he was raised on the third day in accordance with the scriptures; that he appeared to Cephas, then to the Twelve. After that, he appeared to more than five hundred brothers at once, most of whom are still living, though some have fallen asleep. After that he appeared to James, then to all the apostles. Last of all, as to one born abnormally, he appeared to me. For I am the least of the apostles, not fit to be called an apostle, because I persecuted the church of God. But by the grace of God I am what I am, and his grace to me has not been ineffective. (1 Corinthians 15:3–10)

The Resurrection
By Paul Gustave Doré (1866)

After the sabbath, as the first day of the week was dawning,
Mary Magdalene and the other Mary came to see the tomb.
(Matthew 28:1)

Induction: White Light

Start by finding a comfortable position. If you are sitting, have your feet grounded to the floor. If you are lying down, wriggle your feet and toes for comfort. Rest your arms and hands in a comfortable position, either on your lap or by your side, with hands open, closed, in prayer position, or whatever feels easiest for you. Now take three long, deep breaths, slowly breathing in and out from your lower belly area, in through your nose, and out through your mouth. Gently begin to close your eyes, and let yourself soften completely by releasing areas of tension and any negative energies. Imagine that all the stress you harbor is now leaving your body. Now imagine a pure white light entering your body at the top of your head. It can be either a wide fluorescent type, or if you like, a laser beam. Either way, it is directed at you personally and originates far away in the universe. It travels faster than light years and with exact precision, breaking through all tiny holes in the cosmos. Such are very rare openings that we'll call God's grace. It is the light of Jesus Christ and his Father. They both know you by name, and the light that is shining is their infinite love extended to you.

This light now proceeds to immerse your body starting from the top of your head, working your way slowly downward, moving to your neck area, throughout your shoulders, arms, and fingers, then down your torso, to your legs and toes. Feel the light consuming all your tension and floating it right out of you through your feet. All the negative energies, physical illnesses, and psychological struggles now exit your body. You may want to linger the light in any area you may have problems with. Now keep breathing, and as you exhale, let your body relax even more. Imagine all your muscles melting into total surrender and all negativity leaving your body. Now clear your mind, free your thoughts, and focus on my voice. You are going to be meeting with the resurrected Jesus on this day, at the open tomb of Joseph of Arimathea.

Context

Envision that you are traveling back in time two thousand years ago to Israel in the Middle East. The Roman Empire has held control for close to a century, and Pontius Pilate is the current Roman governor. Herod Antipas is tetrarch of Galilee in the province of Judea, and although he is Jewish, he is appointed by Rome to keep the Israelites in place. The high priest of the

Jewish temple is Calipas, and he desperately needs to keep peace and order among the Jews. Pilate has sentenced Jesus to be crucified, and there is still unrest in the streets, and Jesus's followers are lying low.

The Synoptic gospels state that upon resurrection on Sunday morning, Jesus first appeared to Mary Magdalene, Mary the mother of James, Joanna, and Salome, but John places Mary Magdalene alone at the empty open tomb. Luke and Mark mention a short meeting with the Lord by two of the disciples on the road to Emmaus. And all four gospels state that Jesus met with the twelve disciples in Jerusalem in the upper room and then again in Galilee.

Now imagine that it is early Sunday morning and you are on your way to the tomb with the women. The dew from the night is still lingering in the air. As the sun is just beginning to show on the horizon, the fragrance of the wildflowers smells so sweet. The women are still shaken and traumatized from the events on Friday and terribly heartbroken. You're carrying spices and herbs, hoping to anoint the body of Jesus with them, but the tomb is now empty.

> But at daybreak on the first day of the week they took the spices they had prepared and went to the tomb. They found the stone rolled away from the tomb; but when they entered, they did not find the body of the Lord Jesus. While they were puzzling over this, behold, two men in dazzling garments appeared to them. They were terrified and bowed their faces to the ground. They said to them, "Why do you seek the living one among the dead? He is not here, but he has been raised. (Luke 24:1–6)

But as the women return to the tomb, you're mesmerized by the two figures and realize that one of them is Jesus. He motions to you to sit and talk with him. He asks you to speak your heart.

(Take a long pause of three to five minutes.)

Reorientation

Now the scene begins to fade away, but his message lingers on in your heart and with all who honor him. Give thanks to God, and show gratitude for all that you are, the wondrous life and love that you have around you. When you are ready to leave your peaceful place, you can begin to reawaken your body and mind. Feel your muscles reawakening as you take note of your surroundings and slowly return to the present. Wiggle your fingers, and open and close your hands a few times. Wiggle your toes, and flex your ankles. Begin to move your arms and legs, and when you are ready, slowly reopen your eyes. Stretch if you desire to, feeling your body becoming fully awake. Now take a moment to sit quietly as you reawaken completely and further ponder the experience.

The Ascension of Jesus to Heaven
Second Glorious Mystery
Fruit of the Mystery: Hope and Desire for Heaven

The ascension of Jesus is the departure of Christ from earth into heaven to reside in the presence of God. Although the gospel of John made references to the ascension, the gospel of Luke and Acts (both written by the same person) include detailed accounts. In both books, the apostles foretold of the coming of the Holy Spirit that will descend on them. Luke and Acts describe similar events but present different chronologies. Luke places it on the same day as the Resurrection but Acts forty days afterward. Today most Christians celebrate the ascension forty days after the Resurrection, which is always on a Thursday. The Christian holiday of Pentecost is celebrated fifty days (seven weeks) from Easter Sunday, the tenth day after ascension Thursday, which itself is forty days from Easter.

> And he said to them, "Thus it is written that the Messiah would suffer and rise from the dead on the third day and that repentance, for the forgiveness of sins, would be preached in his name to all the nations, beginning from Jerusalem. You are witnesses of these things. And behold I am sending the promise of my Father upon you; but stay in the city until you are clothed with power from on high." Then he led them out as far as Bethany, raised his hands, and blessed them. As he blessed them he parted from them and was taken up to heaven. They did him homage and then returned to Jerusalem with great joy, and they were continually in the temple praising God. (Luke 24:46–53)

The Ascension
By Paul Gustave Doré (1866)

Go, therefore, and make disciples of all nations, baptizing them in the name of the Father, and of the Son, and of the holy Spirit. (Matthew 28:19)

Induction: White Light

Start by finding a comfortable position. If you are sitting, have your feet grounded to the floor. If you are lying down, wriggle your feet and toes for comfort. Rest your arms and hands in a comfortable position, either on your lap or by your side, with hands open, closed, in prayer position, or whatever feels easiest for you. Now take three long, deep breaths, slowly breathing in and out from your lower belly area, in through your nose, out through your mouth. Gently begin to close your eyes and let yourself soften completely by releasing areas of tension and any negative energies. Imagine that all the stress you harbor is now leaving your body. Now imagine a pure white light entering your body at the top of your head. It can be either a wide fluorescent type, or if you like, a laser beam. Either way, it is directed at you personally and originates far away in the universe. It travels faster than light years and with exact precision, breaking through all tiny holes in the cosmos, such are very rare openings that we'll call God's grace. It is the light of Jesus Christ and his Father. They both know you by name, and the light that is shining is their infinite love extended to you.

This light now proceeds to immerse your body, starting from the top of your head and working its way slowly downward, moving to your neck area, throughout your shoulders, arms, and fingers, then down your torso, to your legs and toes. Feel the light consuming all your tension and floating it right out of you through your feet. All the negative energies, physical illnesses, and psychological struggles now exit your body. You may want to linger the light in any area that you may have problems with. Now keep breathing, and as you exhale, let your body relax even more. Imagine all your muscles melting into total surrender and all negativity leaving your body. Now clear your mind, free your thoughts, and focus on my voice. You are going to be meeting with Jesus and his eleven apostles just outside of Jerusalem at the Mount of Olives near Bethany, a Sabbath's day journey northeast of the city.

Context

Envision that you are traveling back in time two thousand years ago to Israel in the Middle East. The Roman Empire has held control for close to a century, and Pontius Pilate is the current Roman governor. Herod Antipas is tetrarch of Galilee in the province of Judea, and although he is Jewish, he is appointed by Rome to keep the Israelites in place. The high priest of the

Jewish temple is Calipas, and he desperately needs to keep peace and order among the Jews. Pilate has sentenced Jesus to be crucified, and there is still unrest in the streets. Jesus's followers are lying low. The resurrected Jesus has appeared to the apostles and others throughout the forty days that He walked the earth.

All four gospels mention the ascension of Jesus. Luke and Acts offer a similar narrative, but with different chronologies. Luke places the event on the same day as the resurrection, and Acts, forty days later. The Feast of the Ascension is now celebrated on the fortieth day of Easter, always a Thursday

Jesus, while in the company of the disciples, is taken up into heaven after instructing them to remain in Jerusalem until the Holy Spirit descends. Two men in white appear to say that he will return one day. Various epistles of the New Testament also refer to an ascension of Christ, equating it with the post-resurrection exultation of Jesus to the right hand of God.

> When they had gathered together they asked him, "Lord, are you at this time going to restore the kingdom to Israel?" He answered them, "It is not for you to know the times or seasons that the Father has established by his own authority. But you will receive power when the holy Spirit comes upon you, and you will be my witnesses in Jerusalem, throughout Judea and Samaria, and to the ends of the earth." When he had said this, as they were looking on, he was lifted up, and a cloud took him from their sight. While they were looking intently at the sky as he was going, suddenly two men dressed in white garments stood beside them. They said, "Men of Galilee, why are you standing there looking at the sky? This Jesus who has been taken up from you into heaven will return in the same way as you have seen him going into heaven." (Acts 1:6–11)

Now imagine that you are there on the Mount of Olives with the apostles. It is forty days after Jesus rose from the dead. The early-morning dew from the night is still lingering in the air. As the sun is just beginning to show on the horizon, the sweet fragrance of the olive trees seem to consume you. This location is the highest point in the surrounding area—three hundred feet above the Temple Mount—and the panoramic view of the second temple site in Old Jerusalem is breathtaking. Jesus appears and talks with each of the apostles. Then he turns to you, reaches out his hand to you, and asks you personally to spread his word.

(Take a long pause of three to five minutes.)

Reorientation

Now the scene begins to fade away, but his message lingers on in your heart and with all who honor him. Give thanks to God, and show gratitude for all that you are, the wondrous life and love that you have around you. When you are ready to leave your peaceful place, you can begin to reawaken your body and mind. Feel your muscles reawakening as you take note of your surroundings and slowly return to the present. Wiggle your fingers, and open and close your hands a few times. Wiggle your toes, and flex your ankles. Begin to move your arms and legs, and when you are ready, slowly reopen your eyes. Stretch if you desire to, feeling your body becoming fully awake. Now take a moment to sit quietly as you reawaken completely and further ponder the experience.

The Descent of the Holy Spirit
Third Glorious Mystery
Fruit of the Mystery: Holy Wisdom to Know Truth

The Christian Pentecost is based on the New Testament, as the descent of the Holy Spirit upon the apostles and other followers of Jesus Christ, which was foretold by Jesus prior. It is thought of by some Christians as the birth of the church. However, Pentecost is the Greek name for the Jewish Shavuot, or Festival of Weeks from the Old Testament (Exodus 34:22, Deuteronomy 16:10), the Festival of Reaping (Exodus 23:16), and Day of the First Fruits (Numbers 28:26). Tradition holds that the descent of the Holy Spirit took place in the Upper Room, or Cenacle, while the apostles were together celebrating the Jewish Shavuot.

> When the time for Pentecost was fulfilled, they were all in one place together. And suddenly there came from the sky a noise like a strong driving wind, and it filled the entire house in which they were. Then there appeared to them tongues as of fire, which parted and came to rest on each one of them. And they were all filled with the holy Spirit and began to speak in different tongues, as the Spirit enabled them to proclaim. Now there were devout Jews from every nation under heaven staying in Jerusalem. At this sound, they gathered in a large crowd, but they were confused because each one heard them speaking in his own language. They were astounded, and in amazement they asked, "Are not all these people who are speaking Galileans? Then how does each of us hear them in his own native language? (Acts 2:1–8)

Jesus and the Disciples Going to Emmaus
By Paul Gustave Doré (1866)

Now that very day two of them were going to a village
seven miles from Jerusalem called Emmaus. (Luke 24:13)

Induction: White Light

Start by finding a comfortable position. If you are sitting, have your feet grounded to the floor. If you are lying down, wriggle your feet and toes for comfort. Rest your arms and hands in a comfortable position, either on your lap or by your side, with hands open, closed, in prayer position, or whatever feels easiest for you. Now take three long, deep breaths, slowly breathing in and out from your lower belly area, in through your nose, out through your mouth. Gently begin to close your eyes, and let yourself soften completely by releasing areas of tension and any negative energies. Imagine that all the stress you harbor is now leaving your body. Now imagine a pure white light entering your body at the top of your head. It can be either a wide fluorescent type, or if you like, a laser beam. Either way, it is directed at you personally and originates far away in the universe. It travels faster than light years and with exact precision, breaking through all the tiny holes in the cosmos. Such are very rare openings that we'll call God's grace. It is the light of Jesus Christ and His Father. They both know you by name, and the light that is shining is their infinite love extended to you.

This light now proceeds to immerse your body, starting from the top of your head, working your way slowly downward, moving to your neck area, throughout your shoulders, arms, and fingers, then down your torso, to your legs and toes. Feel the light consuming all your tension and floating it right out of you through your feet. All the negative energies, physical illnesses, and psychological struggles now exit your body. You may want to linger the light in any area that you may have problems with. Now keep breathing, and as you exhale, let your body relax even more. Imagine all your muscles melting into total surrender and all negativity leaving your body. Now clear your mind, free your thoughts, and focus on my voice. You are going to be meeting with the resurrected Jesus and the eleven apostles in the Upper Room in Old Jerusalem.

Context

Envision that you are traveling back in time two thousand years ago to Israel in the Middle East. The Roman Empire has held control for close to a century, and Pontius Pilate is the current Roman governor. He has recently sentenced Jesus to be crucified, and there is still unrest in the streets. Jesus's followers are lying low. The resurrected Jesus has appeared to the apostles and others throughout the forty days that he walked the earth. They were told that they would receive a spirit from heaven soon after His ascension. It is now the tenth day after ascension Thursday.

Pentecost Sunday is sometimes described by Christians as the "birthday of the church." It is the old Greek and Latin name for the Jewish Festival of Weeks found in the Hebrew Bible, and Jews traditionally read the book of Ruth during that time. Traditional interpretation holds that the descent of the Holy Spirit took place in the Upper Room during the celebration.

> They devoted themselves to the teaching of the apostles and to the communal life, to the breaking of the bread and to the prayers. Awe came upon everyone, and many wonders and signs were done through the apostles. All who believed were together and had all things in common; they would sell their property and possessions and divide them among all according to each one's need. (Acts 2:42–45)

Now imagine that you are there in the Upper Room in Old Jerusalem. It is fifty days after the resurrection. The night is descending, and the Pentecost celebration is at hand. Consider the fruit of the mystery—holy wisdom to know the truth and share with all. You are frightened by the noise and strong winds but are quickly consumed with knowledge and things previously unknown to you. God has revealed much through this descending spirit, and you sit and ponder His message.

(Take a long pause of three to five minutes.)

Reorientation

Now the scene begins to fade away, but his message lingers on in your heart and with all who honor him. Give thanks to God, and show gratitude for all that you are, the wondrous life and love that you have around you. When you are ready to leave your peaceful place, you can begin to reawaken your body and mind. Feel your muscles reawakening as you take note of your surroundings and slowly return to the present. Wiggle your fingers, and open and close your hands a few times. Wiggle your toes, and flex your ankles. Begin to move your arms and legs, and when you are ready, slowly reopen your eyes. Stretch if you desire to, feeling your body becoming fully awake. Now take a moment to sit quietly as you reawaken completely and further ponder the experience.

The Assumption of Mary into Heaven
Fourth Glorious Mystery
Fruit of the Mystery: Grace of a Happy Death and True Devotion to Mary

According to the Catholic Church, the assumption of Mary is also known as the falling asleep of the Blessed Virgin Mary, as her body was incorruptible upon death. In this event, the body of Mary is taken up into heaven at the end of her earthly life. Also called the dormition, the earliest traditions place the end of Mary's life in Jerusalem. Although the gospels do not tell of the assumption, it has been celebrated in the church as early as the fifth century.

> This I declare, brothers: flesh and blood cannot inherit the kingdom of God, nor does corruption inherit incorruption. Behold, I tell you a mystery. We shall not all fall asleep, but we will all be changed, in an instant, in the blink of an eye, at the last trumpet. For the trumpet will sound, the dead will be raised incorruptible, and we shall be changed. For that which is corruptible must clothe itself with incorruptibility, and that which is mortal must clothe itself with immortality. And when this which is corruptible clothes itself with incorruptibility and this which is mortal clothes itself with immortality, then the word that is written shall come about: "Death is swallowed up in victory. Where, O death, is your victory? Where, O death, is your sting?" The sting of death is sin, and the power of sin is the law. But thanks be to God who gives us the victory through our Lord Jesus Christ. (1 Corinthians 15:50–57)

The Sermon on the Mount
By Paul Gustave Doré (1866)

While he was still speaking to the crowds, his mother and
his brothers appeared outside, wishing to speak with him.
(Matthew 12:46)

Induction: White Light

Start by finding a comfortable position. If you are sitting, have your feet grounded to the floor. If you are lying down, wriggle your feet and toes for comfort. Rest your arms and hands in a comfortable position, either on your lap or by your side, with hands open, closed, in prayer position, or whatever feels easiest for you. Now take three long, deep breaths, slowly breathing in and out from your lower belly area, in through your nose, out through your mouth. Gently begin to close your eyes and let yourself soften completely by releasing areas of tension and any negative energies. Imagine that all the stress you harbor is now leaving your body. Now imagine a pure white light entering your body at the top of your head. It can be either a wide fluorescent type, or if you like, a laser beam. Either way, it is directed at you personally and originates far away in the universe. It travels faster than light years and with exact precision, breaking through all the tiny holes in the cosmos. Such are very rare openings that we'll call God's grace. It is the light of Jesus Christ and His Father. They both know you by name, and the light that is shining is their infinite love extended to you.

This light now proceeds to immerse your body, starting from the top of your head, working its way slowly downward, moving to your neck area, throughout your shoulders, arms, and fingers, then down your torso, to your legs and toes. Feel the light consuming all your tension and floating it right out of you through your feet. All the negative energies, physical illnesses, and psychological struggles now exit your body. You may want to linger the light in any area you may have problems with. Now keep breathing, and as you exhale, let your body relax even more. Imagine all your muscles melting into total surrender and all negativity leaving your body. Now clear your mind, free your thoughts, and focus on my voice. You are going to be meeting with Mary and her companions near Ephesus, at the site of her rise into heaven.

Context

Envision that you are traveling back in time two thousand years ago to Israel in the Middle East. The Roman Empire has held control for close to a century, and Pontius Pilate is the current Roman governor. He has recently sentenced Jesus to be crucified, and there is still unrest in the streets. Jesus's followers are lying low. The resurrected Jesus has appeared to the apostles and others throughout the forty days that he walked the earth and the Holy Spirit descended on them at Pentecost.

The Catholic Church teaches the doctrine as dogma, that the Virgin Mary, *having completed the course of her earthly life, was assumed body and soul into heavenly glory,* as defined in 1950 by Pope Pius XII. It is referred to as the dormition by the Eastern Catholic Church and today is celebrated by both churches on August 15.

This dogma is supported from the Book of Genesis. *"I will put enmity between you and the woman, and between your offspring and hers; They will strike at your head, while you strike at their heel"* (Genesis 3:15).

It was later reflected in 1 Corinthians. "And when this which is corruptible clothes itself with incorruptibility and this which is mortal clothes itself with immortality, then the word that is written shall come about: Death is swallowed up in victory" (1 Corinthians 15:54).

Tradition holds that this event took place near Ephesus, where Mary spent her last years with some of the women who followed her son. Consider the fruit of the mystery—grace of a happy death and devotion to Mary. Now imagine you are there with Mary and her companions in her last days on earth. She asks you to sit with her and speak your heart.

(Take a long pause of three to five minutes.)

Reorientation

Now the scene begins to fade away, but the message lingers on in your heart and with all who honor him. Give thanks to God, and show gratitude for all that you are, the wondrous life and love that you have around you. When you are ready to leave your peaceful place, you can begin to reawaken your body and mind. Feel your muscles reawakening as you take note of your surroundings and slowly return to the present. Wiggle your fingers, and open and close your hands a few times. Wiggle your toes and flex your ankles. Begin to move your arms and legs, and when you are ready, slowly reopen your eyes. Stretch if you desire to, feeling your body becoming fully awake. Now take a moment to sit quietly as you reawaken completely and further ponder the experience.

Mary Is Crowned as Queen of Heaven and Earth
Fifth Glorious Mystery
Fruit of the Mystery: Perseverance and Crown of Glory

The coronation of Mary is not noted in the four gospels, although the Catholic Church defends the glorious event from scripture based on passages in the Song of Songs (4:8), Psalms (45:11–12), and Revelation. It arose in the church as veneration to Mary, as Marian devotions gradually increased through the Middle Ages. However, the belief in Mary as queen of heaven was not obtained as being papally sanctioned until 1954 with Pope Pius XII. The event signifies the final episode in the life of the Blessed Mother.

> A great sign appeared in the sky, a woman clothed with the sun, with the moon under her feet, and on her head a crown of twelve stars. She was with child and wailed aloud in pain as she labored to give birth. Then another sign appeared in the sky; it was a huge red dragon, with seven heads and ten horns, and on its heads were seven diadems. Its tail swept away a third of the stars in the sky and hurled them down to the earth. Then the dragon stood before the woman about to give birth, to devour her child when she gave birth. She gave birth to a son, a male child, destined to rule all the nations with an iron rod. Her child was caught up to God and his throne. The woman herself fled into the desert where she had a place prepared by God, that there she might be taken care of for twelve hundred and sixty days. Then war broke out in heaven; Michael and his angels battled against the dragon. The dragon and its angels fought back, but they did not prevail and there was no longer any place for them in heaven. (Revelation 12:1–8)

The Crucifixion
By Paul Gustave Doré (1866)

When Jesus saw his mother and the disciple there whom he loved, he said to his mother, "Woman, behold, your son." (John 19:26)

Induction: White Light

Start by finding a comfortable position. If you are sitting, have your feet grounded to the floor. If you are lying down, wriggle your feet and toes for comfort. Rest your arms and hands in a comfortable position, either on your lap or by your side, with hands open, closed, in prayer position, or whatever feels easiest for you. Now take three long, deep breaths, slowly breathing in and out from your lower belly area, in through your nose, out through your mouth. Gently begin to close your eyes and let yourself soften completely by releasing areas of tension and any negative energies. Imagine that all the stress you harbor is now leaving your body. Now imagine a pure white light entering your body at the top of your head. It can be either a wide fluorescent type, or if you like, a laser beam. Either way, it is directed at you personally and originates far away in the universe. It travels faster than light years and with exact precision, breaking through all the tiny holes in the cosmos. Such are very rare openings that we'll call God's grace. It is the light of Jesus Christ and His Father. They both know you by name, and the light that is shining is their infinite love extended to you.

This light now proceeds to immerse your body starting from the top of your head, working your way slowly downward, moving to your neck area, throughout your shoulders, arms, and fingers, then down your torso, to your legs and toes. Feel the light consuming all your tension and floating it right out of you through your feet. All the negative energies, physical illnesses, and psychological struggles now exit your body. You may want to linger the light in any area that you may have problems with. Now keep breathing, and as you exhale, let your body relax even more. Imagine all your muscles melting into total surrender and all negativity leaving your body. Now clear your mind, free your thoughts, and focus on my voice. You are going to be meeting with Mary and her companions near Ephesus, at the site of her rise into heaven.

Context

Envision that you are traveling back in time two thousand years ago to Israel in the Middle East. The Roman Empire has held control for close to a century, and Pontius Pilate is the current Roman governor. He has recently sentenced Jesus to be crucified, and there is still unrest in the streets. Jesus's followers are lying low. The resurrected Jesus has appeared to the apostles and others throughout the forty days that he walked the earth, and the Holy Spirit descended on them at Pentecost.

The Catholic Church teaches the doctrine as dogma, that the Virgin Mary, *having completed the course of her earthly life, was assumed body and soul into heavenly glory,* as defined in 1950 by Pope Pius XII and is referred to as the dormition by the Eastern Catholic Church. Today it is celebrated by both churches on August 15.

This dogma is supported from the book of Genesis. "I will put enmity between you and the woman, and between your offspring and hers; They will strike at your head, while you strike at their heel" (Genesis 3:15).

It was later reflected in 1 Corinthians. "And when this which is corruptible clothes itself with incorruptibility and this which is mortal clothes itself with immortality, then the word that is written shall come about: Death is swallowed up in victory" (1 Corinthians 15:54).

Tradition holds that this event took place near Ephesus, where Mary spent her last years with some of the women who followed her son. Consider the fruit of the mystery—grace of a happy death and devotion to Mary. Now imagine you are there with Mary and her companions in her last days on earth. She asks you to sit with her and speak your heart.

(Take a long pause of three to five minutes.)

Reorientation

Now the scene begins to fade away, but the message lingers on in your heart and with all who honor him. Give thanks to God, and show gratitude for all that you are, the wondrous life and love that you have around you. When you are ready to leave your peaceful place, you can begin to reawaken your body and mind. Feel your muscles reawakening as you take note of your surroundings and slowly return to the present. Wiggle your fingers, and open and close your hands a few times. Wiggle your toes, and flex your ankles. Begin to move your arms and legs, and when you are ready, slowly reopen your eyes. Stretch if you desire to, feeling your body becoming fully awake. Now take a moment to sit quietly as you reawaken completely and further ponder the experience.

6

The Luminous Mysteries

Stairway to Heaven Induction Scripts
Theme: Peace and Salvation

The Baptism in the Jordan
The Wedding at Cana
The Proclamation of the Kingdom
The Transfiguration
The Institution of the Eucharist

The luminous mysteries are a recent addition to the rosary from Pope John Paul II, which was debuted in 2002 with his Apostolic Letter, *Rosarium Virginis Mariae* (see appendix). These "mysteries of light," as Pope John Paul put it, are events that emerge through the three years of Jesus's public ministry, as he proclaimed his gospel. And when he knew his time was coming to an end, he instructed his apostles to bring it to the world. The events reflect on fruits such as peace and salvation, of course, Christ's main message, but also on practical application for evangelization. These events eventually transitioned into the Catholic Church, such as baptism, marriage, holy orders, confirmation, and communion with God. The focus on these events are on Jesus and His gospel that eventually became His church.

Psalm 103
Praise of Divine Goodness

Of David.
Bless the Lord, my soul;
all my being, bless his holy name!
Bless the Lord, my soul;
and do not forget all his gifts,
Who pardons all your sins,
and heals all your ills,
Who redeems your life from the pit,
and crowns you with mercy and compassion,
Who fills your days with good things,
so your youth is renewed like the eagle's.
The Lord does righteous deeds
brings justice to all the oppressed.
He made known his ways to Moses,
to the Israelites his deeds.
Merciful and gracious is the Lord,
slow to anger, abounding in mercy.
He will not always accuse,
and nurses no lasting anger;
He has not dealt with us as our sins merit,
nor requited us as our wrongs deserve.
For as the heavens tower over the earth,
so his mercy towers over those who fear him.
As far as the east is from the west,
so far has he removed our sins from us.
As a father has compassion on his children,
so the Lord has compassion on those who fear him.
For he knows how we are formed,
remembers that we are dust.
As for man, his days are like the grass;
he blossoms like a flower in the field.

A wind sweeps over it and it is gone;
its place knows it no more.
But the Lord's mercy is from age to age,
toward those who fear him.
His salvation is for the children's children
of those who keep his covenant,
and remember to carry out his precepts.
The Lord has set his throne in heaven;
his dominion extends over all.
Bless the Lord, all you his angels,
mighty in strength, acting at his behest,
obedient to his command.
Bless the Lord, all you his hosts,
his ministers who carry out his will.
Bless the Lord, all his creatures
everywhere in his domain.
Bless the Lord, my soul!

The Baptism in the Jordan
First Luminous Mystery
Fruit of the Mystery: Openness to the Holy Spirit

The baptism of Jesus by his cousin John marks the beginning of his public ministry. This event sheds light on the importance of John the Baptist and his message of repentance for salvation. John truly ushered in the new era for Jesus to lay his gospel out. The Jordan River was already symbolic to the Israelites from Old Testament writings. Elijah ascended at the Jordan, Elisha practiced his ministry along the river, and the Israelites passed through the river to get to the Promised Land. Directly after the baptism of Jesus in the Jordan, he journeys into the desert for forty days of temptation before beginning his ministry.

> Then Jesus came from Galilee to John at the Jordan to be baptized by him. John tried to prevent him, saying, "I need to be baptized by you, and yet you are coming to me?" Jesus said to him in reply, "Allow it now, for thus it is fitting for us to fulfill all righteousness." Then he allowed him. After Jesus was baptized, he came up from the water and behold, the heavens were opened [for him], and he saw the Spirit of God descending like a dove [and] coming upon him. And a voice came from the heavens, saying, "This is my beloved Son, with whom I am well pleased." (Matthew 3:13–17)

The Baptism of Jesus
By Paul Gustave Doré (1866)

It happened in those days that Jesus came from Nazareth of Galilee and was baptized in the Jordan by John. (Mark 1:9)

Induction: Stairway to Heaven

Start by finding a comfortable position. If you are sitting, have your feet grounded to the floor. If you are lying down, wriggle your feet and toes for comfort. Rest your arms and hands in a comfortable position, either on your lap or by your side, with hands open, closed, in prayer position, or whatever feels easiest for you. Now take three long, deep breaths, slowly breathing in and out from your lower belly area, in through your nose, out through your mouth. Gently begin to close your eyes, and let yourself soften completely by releasing areas of tension and any negative energies. Imagine that all the stress you harbor is now leaving your body. Imagine you are lying or sitting on the beach. The day is warm but with a few clouds in the sky, and you begin to drift off to sleep. As you awaken, you notice something that resembles a stairway appearing. It's coming down from the clouds, like an escalator into the sky, perhaps a Jacob's ladder to heaven. It is directed at you personally and originates far away in the universe. It is the staircase to Jesus Christ and His Father. They both know you by name. The stairs are shining like gold, and it is God's grace extended to you to climb up.

Now silently count up with me in your mind as you begin to climb the stairs to heaven, and as you do, all tension and worry you have simply dissolve. One, the day is perfect. Two, the sun is so warm against your skin. Three, you seem to just float up those stairs, four, as if something was lifting you. Five, all the negative energies leave your body. Six, all worries disappear, and seven, you're so excited to see Grandma, eight, as you float right into the clouds. Nine, you are so happy floating in those clouds. Ten, keep breathing and as you exhale let your body relax even more. Imagine all your muscles melting into total surrender and all the negativity leaving you. Now clear your mind, free your thoughts, and focus on my voice. You are going to be meeting with Jesus and John the Baptist today/tonight on the shores of the Jordan River.

Context

Envision that you are traveling back in time two thousand years ago to Israel in the Middle East. The Roman Empire has held control for close to a century, and Pontius Pilate is the current Roman governor. Herod Antipas is tetrarch of Galilee in the province of Judea, and although he is Jewish, he is appointed by Rome to keep the Israelites in place. Times are tense, with

the Jewish people being persecuted as they continue to pray for the coming of their long-prophesied messiah.

Imagine today that you are at the shores of the Jordan River in Palestine. It is midday, the sun is shining, and the day is tepid. The river, traditionally a very sacred place for the Israelites, runs vertically, about a hundred miles between the Sea of Galilee and the Dead Sea in Judea. Today there are hundreds of people flocking to hear the Baptist and get baptized with water. The cool blue water is running along the eastern shoreline, amid the deserts between Galilee and Samaria. It is so peaceful watching the sky fade into the river along the horizon. The prophet John is there, an Essene, the son of Elizabeth and Zacharias, both from the house of Aaron—Aaron, who was the birth brother to Moses. The Essenes, a cult of the second temple Judaism, lived a life of ascetic mysticism and strongly believed in the coming of the Messiah, who they believed would bring salvation to Israel.

John was prophesied to herald in the coming of the Messiah. This revelation in the Jordan signifies the beginning of Jesus's public ministry and was long ago foretold in the Old Testament by the Prophet Isaiah.

> A voice cries out: In the wilderness prepare the way of the Lord! Make straight in the wasteland a highway for our God! Every valley shall be lifted up, every mountain and hill made low; The rugged land shall be a plain, the rough country, a broad valley. Then the glory of the Lord shall be revealed, and all people shall see it together; for the mouth of the Lord has spoken. (Isaiah 40:3–5)

In Catholic teachings, baptism signifies the liberation from both sin, and its instigator, the devil, and necessary for salvation, as based on Jesus's words in the gospel of John. "Truly, truly, I say to you, unless one is born of water and the Spirit, he cannot enter into the Kingdom of God" (John 3:5).

The Spirit now descends upon Jesus in the form of a dove, and filled with the Holy Spirit, he begins to leave the crowd heading toward the Judean desert, where he will fast for forty days. But now John is moving toward you, motioning you to come into the water, and so you go. As he reaches for you, he asks you to repent, and then dips you into the water. As you come up, he says, "I am baptizing you with water, for repentance, but the one who is coming after me is mightier than I. I am not worthy to carry his sandals. He will baptize you with the Holy Spirit and fire" (Matthew 3:11). Now ponder for a few moments on what this scene brings to you today!

Reorientation

Now the scene begins to fade away, but his message lingers on in your heart and with all who honor him. Give thanks to God, and show gratitude for all that you are, the wondrous life and love that you have around you. When you are ready to leave your peaceful place, you can begin to reawaken your body and mind. Feel your muscles reawakening as you take note of your surroundings and slowly return to the present. Wiggle your fingers, and open and close your hands a few times. Wiggle your toes, and flex your ankles. Begin to move your arms and legs, and when you are ready, slowly reopen your eyes. Stretch if you desire to, feeling your body becoming fully awake. Now take a moment to sit quietly as you reawaken completely and further ponder the experience.

The Wedding at Cana
Second Luminous Mystery
Fruit of the Mystery: To Jesus through Mary

The transformation of water into wine at the Cana wedding is the first documented miracle that Jesus performed publicly. John's gospel has the only account, which tells of the couple running out of wine. The significance in this event, aside from it being the first miracle, is that his mother Mary, who was attending the wedding with him, requested that Jesus help out in the situation. This signifies the first intervention of Mary, which would later become a strong defense for the development of the doctrine of the intersession of Mary, and the Marian devotions, within the Catholic Church.

> Now there were six stone water jars there for Jewish ceremonial washings, each holding twenty to thirty gallons. Jesus told them, "Fill the jars with water." So they filled them to the brim. Then he told them, "Draw some out now and take it to the headwaiter." So they took it. And when the headwaiter tasted the water that had become wine, without knowing where it came from (although the servers who had drawn the water knew), the headwaiter called the bridegroom and said to him, "Everyone serves good wine first, and then when people have drunk freely, an inferior one; but you have kept the good wine until now." (John 2:6–10)

The Marriage in Cana
By Paul Gustave Doré (1866)

After this, he and his mother, [his] brothers, and his disciples went down to Capernaum and stayed there only a few days. (John 2:12)

Induction: Stairway to Heaven

Start by finding a comfortable position. If you are sitting, have your feet grounded to the floor. If you are lying down, wriggle your feet and toes for comfort. Rest your arms and hands in a comfortable position, either on your lap or by your side, with hands open, closed, in prayer position, or whatever feels easiest for you. Now take three long, deep breaths, slowly breathing in and out from your lower belly area, in through your nose, out through your mouth. Gently begin to close your eyes and let yourself soften completely by releasing areas of tension and any negative energies. Imagine that all the stress you harbor is now leaving your body. Imagine you are lying or sitting on the beach, the day is warm, but with a few clouds in the sky, and you begin to drift off to sleep. As you awaken, you notice something that resembles a stairway appearing. It's coming down from the clouds, like an escalator into the sky, perhaps a Jacob's ladder to heaven. It is directed at you personally and originates far away in the universe. It is the staircase to Jesus Christ and his Father. They both know you by name, the stairs are shining like gold, and it is God's grace extended to you to climb up.

Now silently count up with me in your mind as you begin to climb the stairs to heaven, and as you do, all tension and worry you have simply dissolve. One, the day is perfect. Two, the sun is so warm against your skin. Three, you seem to just float up those stairs, four, as if something was lifting you. Five, all the negative energies leave your body. Six, all worries disappear. Seven, you're so excited to see Grandma, eight, as you float right into the clouds. Nine, you are so happy floating in those clouds. Ten, keep breathing, and as you exhale, let your body relax even more. Imagine all your muscles melting into total surrender and all the negativity leaving you. Now clear your mind, free your thoughts, and focus on my voice. You are going to be meeting with Jesus and his mother Mary at a wedding in Cana.

Context

Envision that you are traveling back in time two thousand years ago to Israel in the Middle East. The Roman Empire has held control for close to a century, and Pontius Pilate is the current Roman governor. Herod Antipas is tetrarch of Galilee in the province of Judea, and although he is Jewish, he is appointed by Rome to keep the Israelites in place. Times are tense, with

the Jewish people being persecuted as they continue to pray for the coming of their long-prophesied messiah.

Today you are at the wedding in Cana with Jesus, his apostles, and his mother Mary. John's gospel is the only one that tells of this important event, portrayed as the first public miracle of Jesus's ministry. Tradition holds that the biblical city of Cana was just a few miles northeast of Nazareth in Galilee.

> On the third day, there was a wedding in Cana in Galilee, and the mother of Jesus was there Jesus and his disciples were also invited to the wedding. When the wine ran short, the mother of Jesus said to him, "They have no wine." Jesus said to her, "Woman, how does your concern affect me? My hour has not yet come." His mother said to the servers, "Do whatever he tells you." (John 2:1–5)

Jesus then instructed the servers to fill the jars with water and then to take some to the headwaiter, and so they did. The gospel of John is the only gospel where this event is described. He uses this as the first of the seven signs that he argues for in his defense for the divinity of Jesus.

> Jesus did this as the beginning of his signs in Cana in Galilee and so revealed his glory, and his disciples began to believe in him. (John 2:11)

Imagine you are there with Jesus and Mary. You are a witness to this important event—such a humble, yet miraculous happening that begins Jesus's public ministry that would eventually change the world. Consider the virtue of the first intercession of Mary to Jesus, the fruit of the wedding at Cana. Now ponder for a few moments on what this scene could bring to you today in your life!

(Take a long pause of three to five minutes.)

Reorientation

Now the scene begins to fade away, but his message lingers on in your heart and with all who honor him. Give thanks to God, and show gratitude for all that you are, the wondrous life and love that you have around you. When you are ready to leave your peaceful place, you can begin to reawaken your body and mind. Feel your muscles reawakening as you take note of your surroundings and slowly return to the present. Wiggle your fingers, and open and close your hands a few times. Wiggle your toes, and flex your ankles. Begin to move your arms and legs, and when you are ready, slowly reopen your eyes. Stretch if you desire to, feeling your body becoming fully awake. Now take a moment to sit quietly as you reawaken completely and further ponder the experience.

The Proclamation of the Kingdom
Third Luminous Mystery
Fruit of the Mystery: Repentance and Trust in God

The concept of the kingdom of God(s) was common at the time of Jesus with both monotheistic and polytheistic religions, although uttering the word God was frowned upon in early Judaism. Jesus replaced it with heaven with his claim that it had arrived with him. This drew criticism from the Jewish priests as it insinuated that he was the Messiah, which they refused to accept and eventually put him to death for. The kingdom of God or heaven being at hand was mentioned at Christ's baptism in the Jordan, at the Sermon on the Mount, and in Nazareth when he claimed that the scripture passage of Isaiah was fulfilled (Luke 4:21). Jesus believed that the coming of the kingdom was his ministry and that he was sent from God to usher it in. His claim to the right hand of God established him as king. That proclamation brought credit to his good news that forgiveness of sin was available to all who asked for it in his name, but also included a final judgment of humanity.

> At once the Spirit drove him out into the desert, and he remained in the desert for forty days, tempted by Satan. He was among wild beasts, and the angels ministered to him. After John had been arrested, Jesus came to Galilee proclaiming the gospel of God: "This is the time of fulfillment. The kingdom of God is at hand. Repent, and believe in the gospel." As he passed by the Sea of Galilee, he saw Simon and his brother Andrew casting their nets into the sea; they were fishermen. (Mark 1:12–16)

John the Baptist Preaching in the Wilderness
By Paul Gustave Doré (1866)

The next day he saw Jesus coming toward him and said,
"Behold, the Lamb of God, who takes away the sin of the
world." (John 1:29)

Induction: Stairway to Heaven

Start by finding a comfortable position. If you are sitting, have your feet grounded to the floor. If you are lying down, wriggle your feet and toes for comfort. Rest your arms and hands in a comfortable position, either on your lap or by your side, with hands open, closed, in prayer position, or whatever feels easiest for you. Now take three long, deep breaths, slowly breathing in and out from your lower belly area, in through your nose, out through your mouth. Gently begin to close your eyes, and let yourself soften completely by releasing areas of tension and any negative energies. Imagine that all the stress you harbor is now leaving your body. Imagine you are lying or sitting on the beach. The day is warm, but with a few clouds in the sky, and you begin to drift off to sleep. As you awaken, you notice something that resembles a stairway appearing. It's coming down from the clouds, like an escalator into the sky, perhaps a Jacob's ladder to heaven. It is directed at you personally and originates far away in the universe. It is the staircase to Jesus Christ and His Father. They both know you by name, the stairs are shining like gold, and it is God's grace extended to you to climb up.

Now silently count up with me in your mind as you begin to climb the stairs to heaven, and as you do, all tension and worry you have simply dissolve. One, the day is perfect. Two, the sun is so warm against your skin. Three, you seem to just float up those stairs, four, as if something was lifting you. Five, all the negative energies leave your body Six, all worries disappear. Seven, you're so excited to see Grandma, eight, as you float right into the clouds. Nine, you are so happy floating in those clouds. Ten, keep breathing, and as you exhale, let your body relax even more. Imagine all your muscles melting into total surrender and all the negativity leaving you. Now clear your mind, free your thoughts, and focus on my voice. You are going to be meeting with John the Baptist and Jesus on the shores of the Jordan River.

Context

Envision that you are traveling back in time two thousand years ago to Israel in the Middle East. The Roman Empire has held control for close to a century, and Pontius Pilate is the current Roman governor. Herod Antipas is tetrarch of Galilee in the province of Judea, and although he is Jewish, he is appointed by Rome to keep the Israelites in place. Times are tense, with

the Jewish people being persecuted as they continue to pray for the coming of their long-prophesied messiah.

It is at midday, the sun is shining, and the day is tepid. The Jordan River, traditionally a very sacred place for the Israelites, runs vertically, with about one hundred miles from the Sea of Galilee to the Dead Sea in Judea. Today there are hundreds of people flocking to hear John speak and to get baptized with water. Consider the details of your surroundings, the cool blue water running along the eastern shoreline amid the deserts between Galilee and Samaria, and the wondrous scene unraveling in front of you. It is so peaceful watching the sky fade into the river along the horizon.

> Jesus sent out these twelve after instructing them thus, "Do not go into pagan territory or enter a Samaritan town. Go rather to the lost sheep of the house of Israel. As you go, make this proclamation: 'The kingdom of heaven is at hand. Cure the sick, raise the dead, cleanse lepers, drive out demons. Without cost you have received; without cost you are to give.'" (Matthew 10:5–8)

Consider the virtue of gratitude, the fruit of the proclamation of the kingdom of God, such a gift of faith, a phenomenon that would begin Jesus's public ministry. The Holy Spirit descends upon Jesus, and he is sent into the desert for forty days of temptation by the devil. Consider the good news that this happening eventually leaves behind for all of us to live by, repentance, redemption, and salvation. Now ponder for a few moments on what this scene could bring to you today in your life!

(Take a long pause of three to five minutes.)

Reorientation

Now the scene begins to fade away, but His message lingers on in your heart and with all who honor Him. Give thanks to God and show gratitude for all that you are, the wondrous life and love that you have around you. When you are ready to leave your peaceful place, you can begin to reawaken your body and mind. Feel your muscles reawakening as you take note of your surroundings and slowly return to the present. Wiggle your fingers, and open and close your hands a few times. Wiggle your toes and flex your ankles. Begin to move your arms and legs, and when you are ready, slowly reopen your eyes. Stretch if you desire to, feeling your body becoming fully awake. Now take a moment to sit quietly as you reawaken completely and further ponder the experience.

The Transfiguration
Fourth Luminous Mystery
Fruit of the Mystery: Desire for Holiness

The transfiguration event is told in various passages throughout the New Testament when Jesus took Peter, James, and John to an unnamed mountain (thought to be Mount Tabor). The scene is described that Jesus became transfigured and began to radiate with bright light. The prophets Moses and Elijah suddenly appeared next to him, and Jesus talked with them. A loud voice from the cloud said, "This is my beloved Son, with whom I am well pleased; listen to him" (Mark 9:7). The three disciples then fell to the ground in fear, but Jesus approached and touched them, telling them not to be afraid. This metaphysical event supports the identity of Jesus as the Son of God. The significance of this scene is enhanced by the presence of Elijah and Moses, which exalts Jesus to their status with God.

> After six days Jesus took Peter, James, and John his brother, and led them up a high mountain by themselves. And he was transfigured before them; his face shone like the sun and his clothes became white as light. And behold, Moses and Elijah appeared to them, conversing with him. Then Peter said to Jesus in reply, "Lord, it is good that we are here. If you wish, I will make three tents here, one for you, one for Moses, and one for Elijah." While he was still speaking, behold, a bright cloud cast a shadow over them, then from the cloud came a voice that said, "This is my beloved Son, with whom I am well pleased; listen to him." When the disciples heard this, they fell prostrate and were very much afraid. But Jesus came and touched them, saying, "Rise, and do not be afraid." And when the disciples raised their eyes, they saw no one else but Jesus alone. (Matthew 17:1–8)

The Transfiguration
By Paul Gustave Doré (1866)

And behold, two men were conversing with him, Moses and Elijah. (Luke 9:30)

Induction: Stairway to Heaven

Start by finding a comfortable position. If you are sitting, have your feet grounded to the floor. If you are lying down, wriggle your feet and toes for comfort. Rest your arms and hands in a comfortable position, either on your lap or by your side, with hands open, closed, in prayer position, or whatever feels easiest for you. Now take three long, deep breaths, slowly breathing in and out from your lower belly area, in through your nose, out through your mouth. Gently begin to close your eyes and let yourself soften completely by releasing areas of tension and any negative energies. Imagine that all the stress you harbor is now leaving your body. Imagine you are lying or sitting on the beach, the day is warm, but with a few clouds in the sky, and you begin to drift off to sleep. As you awaken, you notice something that resembles a stairway appearing. It's coming down from the clouds, like an escalator into the sky, perhaps a Jacob's ladder to heaven. It is directed at you personally and originates far away in the universe. It is the staircase to Jesus Christ and His Father. They both know you by name, the stairs are shining like gold, and it is God's grace extended to you to climb up.

Now silently count up with me in your mind as you begin to climb the stairs to heaven, and as you do, all tension and worry you have simply dissolve. One, the day is perfect. Two, the sun is so warm against your skin. Three, you seem to just float up those stairs, four, as if something was lifting you. Five, all the negative energies leave your body Six, all worries disappear. Seven, you're so excited to see Grandma, eight, as you float right into the clouds. Nine, you are so happy floating in those clouds. Ten, keep breathing, and as you exhale, let your body relax even more. Imagine all your muscles melting into total surrender and all the negativity leaving you. Now clear your mind, free your thoughts, and focus on my voice. You are going to be meeting with Jesus, Peter, James, and John at the site of the transfiguration.

Context

Envision that you are traveling back in time two thousand years ago to Israel in the Middle East. The Roman Empire has held control for close to a century, and Pontius Pilate is the current Roman governor. Herod Antipas is tetrarch of Galilee in the province of Judea, and although he is Jewish, he is appointed by Rome to keep the Israelites in place. Times are tense, with

the Jewish people being persecuted as they continue to pray for the coming of their long-prophesied messiah.

All three synoptic gospels, Matthew, Mark, and Luke, narrate this event, although none identify the mountain. Christian tradition holds that it is Mount Tabor about ten miles west of the Sea of Galilee that this miraculous happening transpired.

The book of Malachi written a few centuries earlier foretold the return of Elijah. "Behold, I will send you Elijah the prophet before the coming of the great and dreadful day of the Lord: And he shall turn the heart of the fathers to the children, And the heart of the children to their fathers, Lest I come and smite the earth with a curse" (Malachi 4:6).

> After six days Jesus took Peter, James, and John and led them up a high mountain apart by themselves. And he was transfigured before them, and his clothes became dazzling white, such as no fuller on earth could bleach them. Then Elijah appeared to them along with Moses, and they were conversing with Jesus. Then Peter said to Jesus in reply, "Rabbi, it is good that we are here! Let us make three tents: one for you, one for Moses, and one for Elijah." He hardly knew what to say, they were so terrified. Then a cloud came, casting a shadow over them; then from the cloud came a voice, "This is my beloved Son. Listen to him." Suddenly, looking around, they no longer saw anyone but Jesus alone with them. (Mark 9:2–8)

Now ponder the virtue of this mystery—the desire of holiness, the fruit of the transfiguration. Imagine you are there on the mountainside with Jesus and the three apostles. You are a witness to this pivotal moment—the point when Jesus becomes the connection from the physical world to the metaphysical, the bridge between heaven and earth. Consider such a gift of faith, a phenomenon that would later pave the way for Jesus' declaration that he is truly the Son of God. Now ponder for a few moments on what this scene could bring to you today in your life

(Take a long pause of three to five minutes.)

Reorientation

Now the scene begins to fade away, but his message lingers on in your heart and with all who honor him. Give thanks to God and show gratitude for all that you are, the wondrous life and love that you have around you. When you are ready to leave your peaceful place, you can begin to reawaken your body and mind. Feel your muscles reawakening as you take note of your surroundings and slowly return to the present. Wiggle your fingers, and open and close your hands a few times. Wiggle your toes, and flex your ankles. Begin to move your arms and legs, and when you are ready, slowly reopen your eyes. Stretch if you desire to, feeling your body becoming fully awake. Now take a moment to sit quietly as you reawaken completely and further ponder the experience.

The Institution of the Eucharist
Fifth Luminous Mystery
Fruit of the Mystery: Adoration

The institution of the Eucharist is included in various accounts of the New Testament (Matthew, Mark, Luke, Paul). The term *Last Supper* does not appear in the gospels, although there are references to a final meal that Jesus shared with his apostles in Jerusalem before his crucifixion. During the meal, he predicts the betrayal of Judas, foretells of Peter's denials, and tells his followers of his eminent fatal fate. Jesus divides up some bread, prays over it, and hands the pieces of bread to his disciples, saying "this is my body." He then takes a cup of wine, and passes it around, saying "this is my blood of the everlasting covenant, which is poured for many." Finally, according to Paul and Luke, he tells the disciples "do this in remembrance of me." This event has been regarded by many Christians as the institution of the Eucharist. The act was followed by early Christians in celebration of Christ, and the words are still used in the Catholic liturgy during transubstantiation.

> They devoted themselves to the teaching of the apostles and to the communal life, to the breaking of the bread and to the prayers. Awe came upon everyone, and many wonders and signs were done through the apostles. All who believed were together and had all things in common; they would sell their property and possessions and divide them among all according to each one's need. Every day they devoted themselves to meeting together in the temple area and to breaking bread in their homes. They ate their meals with exultation and sincerity of heart, praising God and enjoying favor with all the people. And every day the Lord added to their number those who were being saved. (Acts 2:42–47)

The Last Supper
By Paul Gustave Doré (1866)

Then they went off and found everything exactly as he had told them, and there they prepared the Passover. (Luke 22:13)

Induction: Stairway to Heaven

Start by finding a comfortable position. If you are sitting, have your feet grounded to the floor. If you are lying down, wriggle your feet and toes for comfort. Rest your arms and hands in a comfortable position, either on your lap or by your side, with hands open, closed, in prayer position, or whatever feels easiest for you. Now take three long, deep breaths, slowly breathing in and out from your lower belly area, in through your nose, out through your mouth. Gently begin to close your eyes, and let yourself soften completely by releasing areas of tension and any negative energies. Imagine that all the stress you harbor is now leaving your body. Imagine you are lying or sitting on the beach, the day is warm, but with a few clouds in the sky, and you begin to drift off to sleep. As you awaken, you notice something that resembles a stairway appearing. It's coming down from the clouds, like an escalator into the sky, perhaps a Jacob's ladder to heaven. It is directed at you personally and originates far away in the universe. It is the staircase to Jesus Christ and his Father. They both know you by name, the stairs are shining like gold, and it is God's grace extended to you to climb up.

Now silently count up with me in your mind as you begin to climb the stairs to heaven, and as you do, all tension and worry you have simply dissolve. One, the day is perfect. Two, the sun is so warm against your skin Three, you seem to just float up those stairs, four, as if something was lifting you. Five, all the negative energies leave your body. Six, all worries disappear. Seven, you're so excited to see Grandma, eight, as you float right into the clouds. Nine, you are so happy floating in those clouds. Ten, keep breathing, and as you exhale, let your body relax even more. Imagine all your muscles melting into total surrender and all the negativity leaving you. Now clear your mind, free your thoughts, and focus on my voice. You are going to be meeting with Jesus and his apostles at the last supper in the upper room.

Context

Envision that you are traveling back in time two thousand years ago to Israel in the Middle East. The Roman Empire has held control for close to a century, and Pontius Pilate is the current Roman governor. Herod Antipas is tetrarch of Galilee in the province of Judea, and although he is Jewish, he is appointed by Rome to keep the Israelites in place. Times are tense, with

the Jewish people being persecuted as they continue to pray for the coming of their long-prophesied messiah.

The Last Supper is documented in all four gospels. The Catholic Church's teachings place the origin of the Eucharist at the Last Supper of Jesus Christ with his apostles, at which he is believed to have taken bread and given it to his disciples, telling them to eat of it, because it was his body, and to have taken a cup and given it to them, telling them to drink of it because it was the cup of the covenant of his blood. The early Christians continued this tradition of the breaking of bread as a ceremonial gesture.

> For I received from the Lord what I also handed on to you, that the Lord Jesus, on the night he was handed over, took bread, and, after he had given thanks, broke it and said, "This is my body that is for you. Do this in remembrance of me." In the same way also the cup, after supper, saying, "This cup is the new covenant in my blood. Do this, as often as you drink it, in remembrance of me." (1 Corinthians 11:23–25)

Now ponder this virtue of adoration of the Holy Eucharist, such a gift of faith, the mystery called transubstantiation today, a phenomenon and tradition that would bind Christ's people for the next two thousand years. Consider for a few moments what this scene was like at the Last Supper or with the early Christian groups that practiced it. What could this scene offer you today in your life!

(Take a long pause of three to five minutes.)

Reorientation

Now the scene begins to fade away, but his message lingers on in your heart and with all who honor him. Give thanks to God, and show gratitude for all that you are, the wondrous life and love that you have around you. When you are ready to leave your peaceful place, you can begin to reawaken your body and mind. Feel your muscles reawakening as you take note of your surroundings and slowly return to the present. Wiggle your fingers, and open and close your hands a few times. Wiggle your toes, and flex your ankles. Begin to move your arms and legs, and when you are ready, slowly reopen your eyes. Stretch if you desire to, feeling your body becoming fully awake. Now take a moment to sit quietly as you reawaken completely and further ponder the experience.

Appendix I
Basic Structure of the Rosary

The rosary is begun on the short strand.
It starts with the sign of the cross on the crucifix.

Then comes the Apostles' Creed, still on the crucifix:
I believe in God, the Father almighty, creator of heaven and earth. I believe in Jesus Christ, God's only Son, our Lord, who was conceived by the Holy Spirit, born of the Virgin Mary, suffered under Pontius Pilate, was crucified, died, and was buried; he descended to the dead. On the third day he rose again; he ascended into heaven, he is seated at the right hand of the Father, and he will come to judge the living and the dead. I believe in the Holy Spirit, the holy catholic church, the communion of saints, the forgiveness of sins, the resurrection of the body, and the life everlasting. Amen.

The Lord's Prayer at the first large bead:
Our Father in heaven, hallowed be your name. Your kingdom come, your will be done, on earth as it is in heaven. Give us this day our daily bread, and forgive us our sins as we have forgiven those who have sinned against us. And deliver us from evil. Amen.

The Hail Mary on each of the next three beads:
Hail Mary, full of grace. Our Lord is with you. Blessed are you among women, and blessed is the fruit of your womb, Jesus. Holy Mary, Mother of God. Pray for us sinners, now and at the hour of our death. Amen.

The Glory Be on the next large bead;
Glory be to the Father and the Son and the Holy Spirit, as it was in the beginning, is now, and ever shall be world without end. Amen.

Fatima Decade Prayer often continued from the Glory Be:
O my Jesus, forgive us our sins, save us from the fires of hell, lead all souls to heaven, especially those most in need of thy mercy. Amen.

The praying of the decades follows, repeating the cycle for each mystery:
Announce the mystery.
The Lord's Prayer on the large bead.
The Hail Mary on each of the ten adjacent small beads.
The Glory Be on the space before the next large bead.

To conclude, the Salve Regina:
Hail, holy Queen, Mother of Mercy, our life, our sweetness, and our hope. To you do we cry, poor, banished children of Eve; to you do we send up our sighs, mourning, and weeping in this valley of tears. Turn then, most gracious advocate, your eyes of mercy toward us; and after this our exile, show us the blessed fruit of your womb, Jesus. O clement, O loving, O sweet Virgin Mary. Pray for us, O holy Mother of God, that we may be made worthy of the promises of Christ.

The Loreto Litany often continued from the Salve Regina:
Let us pray; Grant, we beseech thee, O Lord God, that we, your servants, may enjoy perpetual health of mind and body; and by the intercession of the Blessed Mary, ever Virgin, may we be delivered from present sorrow and obtain eternal joy. Through Christ our Lord. Amen.

The sign of the cross.

Appendix II
Dore Illustrations and Scriptural Captions

The Joyful Mysteries

The Annunciation (Isaiah 7:14)
Wise Men Guided by the Star (Matthew 2:2)
The Nativity (Micah 5:1)
The Flight into Egypt (Hosea 11:1)
Jesus with the Doctors (John 7:16)

The Sorrowful Mysteries

The Agony in the Garden (Matthew 26:41)
Jesus Scourged (Matthew 27:26)
The Crown of Thorns (Matthew 27:29)
Jesus Falling Beneath the Cross (Matthew 16:24)
The Erection of the Cross (Mark 15:39)

The Glorious Mysteries

The Resurrection (Matthew 28:1)
The Ascension (Matthew 28:19)
Jesus and the Disciples Going to Emmaus (Luke 24:13)
The Sermon on the Mount (Matthew 12:46)
The Crucifixion (John 19:26)

The Luminous Mysteries

 The Baptism of Jesus (Mark 1:9)
 The Marriage in Cana (John 2:12)
 John the Baptist Preaching in the Wilderness (John 1:29)
 The Transfiguration (Luke 9:30)
 The Last Supper (Luke 22:13)

Appendix III
List of Psalms and Scripture

The Joyful Mysteries
(Isaiah 53:1–12)
(Luke 1:26–33, 1:35–38)
(Luke 1:5–13, 1:39–45)
(Micah 5:1–3, Luke 2:13–15, Matthew 2:1–6)
(Leviticus 12:1–6, Luke 2:25–32)
(Luke 2:41–47, 2:48–49)

The Sorrowful Mysteries
Psalm 143, A Prayer in Distress (Mark 8:27–30)
(Mark 14:33–40, Luke 22:43–45)
(John 18:33–38, 19:1–3)
(John 19:2–4, Mark 15:16–20)
(John 19:10–17, Luke 23:26–29)
(Zechariah 12:10, Luke 23:35–38, Mark 15:34–38)

The Glorious Mysteries
Psalm 70, Prayer for Divine Help
Psalm 112, The Blessings of the Just (Mark 8:27–32)
(1 Corinthians 15:3–10, (uke 24:1–6)
(Luke 24: 46–53, Acts 1:6–11)
(Acts 2:1–8, 2:42–45)
(1 Corinthians 15:50–57, Genesis 3:15, 1 Corinthians 15:54)
(Revelation 12:1–8, Genesis 3:15, 1 Corinthians 15:54)

The Luminous Mysteries

Psalm 103, Praise of Divine Goodness

(Matthew 3:13–17, Isaiah 40:3–5)

(John 2:6–10, 2:1–5, 2:11)

(Mark 1:12–16, Matthew 10:5–8)

(Matthew 17:1–8, Mark 9:2–8)

(Acts 2:42–47, 1 Corinthians 11:23–25)

Appendix IV
The Liturgical Calendar

Advent and Christmas Season (five to six weeks)
The Nativity of our Lord Jesus Christ (Christmas)
Finding Jesus in the Temple (Holy Family Feast/Octave Sunday)
The Baptism in the Jordan (first Sunday after January 6)

Lent and Easter Season (twelve to thirteen weeks)
The Agony of Jesus in the Garden (Holy Thursday)
The Institution of the Eucharist (Holy Thursday)
The Scourging at the Pillar (Good Friday)
Jesus is Crowned with Thorns (Good Friday)
Jesus Carries the Cross (Good Friday)
The Crucifixion of our Lord (Good Friday)
The Resurrection of Jesus Christ (Easter Sunday)
The Ascension of Jesus to Heaven (fortieth day of Easter)
The Descent of the Holy Spirit (fiftieth day of Easter)

Ordinary Time (thirty-three to thirty-four weeks)
The Presentation of Our Lord (February 2)
The Annunciation of the Lord to Mary (March 25)
The Visitation of Mary to Elizabeth (May 31)
The Transfiguration (August 6)
The Assumption of Mary into Heaven (August 15)
Mary is Crowned as Queen of Heaven and Earth (August 22)
The Wedding at Cana (no set date)
Proclamation of the Kingdom (Feast of Christ the King)

Printed in the United States
By Bookmasters